William H. Prescott (1796–1859)
History of the Conquest of Mexico
(1843)

Sir John Elliott is Regius Professor Emeritus of Modern History in the University of Oxford. His many publications on Spain, Europe and the Americas in the Early Modern period include *Imperial Spain, 1469–1716* (1963); *The Old World and the New, 1492–1650* (1970); *The Count-Duke of Olivares* (1986); and *Empires of the Atlantic World*, 1492–1830 (2006). A selection of his essays, *Spain and its World, 1500–1700*, was published in 1989, and a further selection, *Spain, Europe and the Wider World, 1500–1800* appeared in 2009. He was awarded the Wolfson Prize for History in 1986, the Prince of Asturias Prize for the Social Sciences in 1996, and the Balzan Prize for History in 1999. He has received various honours from the Spanish government, and was knighted for his services to history in 1994.

CONTINUUM HISTORIES
The greatest narrative history writing in English

This series is designed to attract a new generation of readers to some of the greatest narrative history ever written. Each volume includes a dramatic episode from a major work of history, prefaced with an introduction by a leading modern authority.

Continuum Histories demonstrate the extraordinary tradition that exists of great history writing in the English language – and that often the best stories are true stories.

Series Editor: Mark Bostridge

History of the
Conquest of Mexico

WILLIAM H. PRESCOTT'S

History of the
Conquest of Mexico

Introduced and selected by
J.H. Elliott

continuum

Published by the Continuum International Publishing Group

The Tower Building	80 Maiden Lane
11 York Road	Suite 704
London	New York
SE1 7NX	NY 10038

www.continuumbooks.com

Introduction and selection copyright © J.H. Elliott, 2009.

First published 2009

British Library Cataloguing-in-Publication Data
A catalogue record for this book is available from the British Library.

ISBN 978-1441-14699-1

Designed and typeset by www.benstudios.co.uk
Printed and bound by The MPG Book Group

CONTENTS

INTRODUCTION

The year 1859 saw the death of the two most famous historians in the English-speaking world. One was Lord Macaulay. The other was William Hickling Prescott, a Boston gentleman-scholar who had first come to the attention of Anglo–American readers with his *History of the Reign of Ferdinand and Isabella* (1838), but sealed his reputation with his *History of the Conquest of Mexico* (1843), and its companion volume, *The History of the Conquest of Peru* (1847). On a visit to the British Isles in 1850 he was everywhere fêted, and Disraeli, on being introduced to Prescott, opened the conversation by asking: 'Pray, are you related to the great American author – the author of the Spanish Histories?' 'I squeezed his arm', recorded Prescott, 'telling him that I could not answer for the greatness, but I was the man himself.'[1]

Prescott's response was characteristically modest. His fame as 'the author of the Spanish Histories', while gratifying, seems to have come to him as something of a surprise. 'Spanish Histories' did not, on the face of it, seem destined to be best-sellers in the Anglo–American world, and Prescott was well aware of his own limitations as a historian, although he also knew his strengths. But there was something improbable

1

about the way in which this wealthy Bostonian, who might have passed his life in the city's literary circles as no more than a cultivated dilettante, discovered both his vocation and his subject, and went on to achieve international renown.

Born in 1796, the son of a judge who had made a fortune at the Massachusetts Bar, he seemed destined to study in his father's footsteps and become a successful lawyer.[2] An accident during his second year at Harvard, however, changed the course of his life. He was struck in the left eye by a crust of bread thrown by a fellow student in the dining hall, and lost the use of it. Not long afterwards, an attack of rheumatic fever weakened his other eye and specialists in England, whom he consulted after recuperating in the Azores, told him that there was no chance of effecting a permanent cure. While he could still read, although with difficulty, he was forced to abandon the prospect of a legal career. This does not seem to have greatly dismayed him, and he continued on his European travels in France and Italy. It was apparently the reading of Gibbon's autobiography that gave him the idea of becoming a historian, but his poor eyesight would make it difficult for him to read and write without human and mechanical assistance. When he returned home to Boston in 1817 he had with him a 'noctograph', a frame with brass wires which guided him along the lines as he wrote with a stylus on carbon paper, to which a sheet of ordinary paper was clamped. This device, which he used throughout his life, enabled him to write without having to read the words he had written – a task that fell to his unfortunate secretaries.

Marrying in 1820, his first task, if he were to turn himself into a scholar and a historian, was to broaden and deepen his reading, and extend his proficiency in classical and modern languages. But German Gothic print proved too much for his weak eyesight, and in 1824 he decided to learn Spanish as a substitute for German.[3] On 13 February 1825 he records the event in the notebooks, or 'Literary Memoranda', in which he would make periodic entries throughout his life: 'I began the study of Spanish December 1, 1824. I have written daily exercises; studied thoroughly Jossé's *Grammar*,' and he follows with a list of the works of Spanish literature he had been reading, including *Don Quijote*, and the history of the conquest of Mexico by the seventeenth-century Spanish historian, Antonio de Solís y Rivadaneyra.[4] The entry in the notebooks is characteristic of the man. Making light of his physical difficulty, and struggling against what he believed to be a natural disposition to indolence, he would pursue a rigid self-discipline, spurred on by his determination to live up to the high moral principles inculcated by his Boston background and his Unitarian upbringing.

The effect of his immersion in Spanish literature was to draw him away from his first intention of working on Italian literature and history, and to shift to Spain instead. This led him, in 1826, to choose as a suitable topic for study the relatively unfamiliar Spain of the late fifteenth century and the joint reigns of Ferdinand and Isabella. He began ordering books from Spain, and built up a network of friends and correspondents who, for the rest of his life, would supply him with transcripts of documents from the Spanish archives. When books and transcripts arrived in Boston he would summarize them on his noctograph, and then carefully digest his notes, committing as much as possible of what he had read to his memory. This became so good that he learnt to compose whole chapters in his mind before committing them in their final form to his noctograph. *The History of the Reign of Ferdinand and Isabella* took ten years to complete, but when it was published at the end of 1837, it was an instant success. Even Prescott's close friends were amazed by the narrative and literary skills displayed in the History, which secured him an international reputation as it found rapidly growing numbers of readers on both sides of the Atlantic.

An account of the conquest of Mexico by Hernán Cortés and his fellow conquistadores would have seemed the natural choice for a new project, as the logical continuation of the story of Spain's rise to greatness under Ferdinand and Isabella. But for some time Prescott, always drawn by literary history, toyed with the notion of writing a life of Molière, and he acquired from France all the books he needed for the task. The extraordinary success of his *Ferdinand and Isabella*, however, encouraged him, in his own words, to 'go on with another subject, which seemed to be a natural continuation of the last, which had the superior advantage of relating to my own quarter of the globe and for which I now possessed eminent advantages for procuring original, unpublished material from Spain… Should I be so fortunate as to obtain them, it will give a new and most authentic basis to the history of a series of brilliant adventures, which, from their relation to my own country cannot fail, thus recommended, to have sufficient interest… Should I get the materials from Spain, I may produce a work of permanent value.'[5]

Prescott's choice of words in explaining his decision to write the *History of the Conquest of Mexico* is revealing. He was attracted to the prospect of continuing what he had already accomplished in his *Ferdinand and Isabella*, the narration of 'a series of brilliant adventures'. Such narration would reveal the human spirit at its most noble and indomitable, and emphasize the vital role played by men and women of character in the onward march of history. This was a theme that would be dear not only to Prescott but to the Boston historians of a slightly younger generation, John Lothrop Motley (1814–77), the author of *The Rise of the Dutch Republic*, and Francis Parkman (1823–93), the great chronicler of the struggle between France and Britain for the domination of North America.[6]

Equally revealing was Prescott's insistence on the importance of a work that would have 'sufficient interest'. The interest, in this instance, would come not only from the character of the personalities involved, and above all that of Cortés himself, but also from the circumstance that the book would be dealing with the history of the western hemisphere, and thus impinge on the history of the future United States, a young republic that would invade Mexico, a still younger republic, three years after the publication of Prescott's *Conquest*. The interest was enhanced, too, by the fact that the story involved a 'grand theme'. The creation and fall of empires, the origins of nations, the progress of liberty and the advance of civilization all provided the kind of 'grand theme' that Prescott and his fellow Boston historians considered essential for the writing of great history.[7] Finally, the use of original sources would confer permanent value, rather than mere ephemeral success, on a book that might otherwise be no more than a retelling, however brilliant, of a relatively familiar story.

In reality, an account of the Spanish conquest of Mexico proved to be ideally suited both to Prescott's idea of history and to his particular gifts. He was heir to the great historical tradition of the eighteenth century, that of Gibbon and William Robertson, the Scottish historian whose *History of America* (1777) was one of the most famous historical works of its age, and whose shadow hovered above Prescott as he wrote. Like Gibbon and Robertson he regarded history as a branch of letters and, like them, he saw himself as an exponent of 'philosophic history', which combined factual accuracy and narrative skill with a determination to discover the underlying causes of events from the standpoint of a society that conceived of history in terms of the continuing improvement of manners and morals, and the progressive advance of civilization, towards the felicitous state it had attained in eighteenth-century Europe.[8]

But if Prescott was the self-conscious heir of the eighteenth century, he was also a member of the generation that experienced the full force of the Romantic movement of the early nineteenth. Romantic historians tended to see the past in terms of great men – of heroic individuals who embodied the spirit of their nation. Daring deeds and sheer force of character enabled these heroes to overcome one obstacle after another as they led their people on the treacherous but upward path that would eventually lead the human race to the full and universal enjoyment of political and spiritual liberty. Romantic history, however, demanded not only the assertion of great moral principles, but also a powerful visual imagination and the capacity to depict historical events with a literary skill that would enable readers to visualize the scene and experience the emotions of the moment as if they were physically present. Not for nothing was Sir Walter Scott the presiding literary genius of this generation.

6

Prescott had already displayed this skill in his *Ferdinand and Isabella*, and the Spanish conquest of Mexico offered him an even greater opportunity for deploying it to the full. In the figure of Cortés he had a hero, who, for all his defects, accomplished a feat that seemed little short of miraculous in overthrowing the mighty Aztec empire with no more than a handful of men. While Cortés symbolized all the energy, confidence and daring of the Spanish people at their moment of greatness, Montezuma, hesitant and pusillanimous, faced him as the representative of a civilization that, in spite of important achievements, was plainly inferior to that of Spain. The story itself was packed with drama – with heroic marches, fiercely contested battles and displays of courage and treachery in equal measure – and had as its backdrop the exotic landscapes of Mexico, with its jungles and volcanoes, and the lake city of Tenochtitlan shimmering in the sunlight. With such a story, and such a setting, Prescott could hardly fail, and he knew it.

All that he needed was sufficient documentary material to give his account the freshness and originality it demanded. By the end of April 1839 he had what he wanted. The President of the Spanish Royal Academy of History, Martín Fernández de Navarrete, not only gave the copyists employed by Prescott full access to the many manuscripts it housed, but also generously offered him transcripts from his own extensive collection. Prescott noted in his Literary Memoranda the recent receipt of 'one large parcel of letters of the MSS., amounting in all to 2500 pp., and consisting of letters of Cortés and the principal actors in his drama, and of other notices and records, hitherto unpublished… Thus, the doubt as to the acquisition of the materials essential to the success of my undertaking is dispelled.'[9] By July he had worked out the ground-plan of the book, but the long introductory section on Aztec civilization – the part that now looks most dated – took him two years of study and writing, and it was not until the summer of 1841 that he was able to embark on the theme that really excited him, the drama of Cortés's march into the interior and the extraordinary succession of events that followed. The last pages were written in July 1843, exactly as he had planned.[10] The book was published a few months later, and took the United States and Europe by storm.

Why was the *Conquest of Mexico* such an instant and immediate success, and why does it continue to be read more than a century and a half after its original publication? Prescott himself, in contemplating the work he had in mind before setting pen to paper, provides a clue to the answer. 'The true way of conceiving the subject', he wrote, 'is, not as a philosophical theme, but as an *epic in prose*, a romance of chivalry… which, while it combines all the picturesque features of the romantic school, is borne onwards on a tide of destiny, like that which broods over the fictions of the Grecian poets; – for surely there is nothing in the compass of Grecian epic or tragic fable, in which the resistless march of *destiny* is more discernible, than in the sad fortunes of the dynasty of Montezuma. – It is, without doubt, the most poetic subject every offered to the pen of the historian.'[11]

An epic in prose. Once he had set the scene, Prescott realized that his readers would be carried along by the sheer excitement of a drama that he could present as unfolding with all the inevitability of a Greek tragedy. As he saw it, it was 'the resistless march of *destiny*' that gave the overthrow of Montezuma's empire its inevitability, and the source of this inevitability was to be found in the character of Aztec civilization itself. The written sources available to him for the study of this civilization were limited, and Mexican archaeology at the time of his writing was still in its infancy. As a result, the picture he could paint of pre-Colombian Mexico was bound to be superficial. While well aware of the achievements of the Aztecs, and impressed by Spanish accounts of Tenochtitlan and the great temple-pyramid – the *teocalli* – at its centre, he could write of Montezuma as having 'the rude intellect of a barbarian'.[12] Even if the emperor's subjects were no longer savages, they were at best 'semi-civilized'.[13] 'The Aztec', he wrote, 'had plainly reached that middle station, as far above the rude races of the New World as it was below the cultivated communities of the Old.'[14] This inferiority to the 'cultivated communities' of the Old World meant that, with the arrival of the Spaniards, Montezuma and his empire were doomed from the start.

That sense of doom pervades Prescott's account of the conquest, giving the story the air of tragic inevitability that he was so anxious to convey to his readers, and that continues to haunt every subsequent retelling of it. Providence tends to play an active part in Prescott's narrative, but underlying his sense of the role of Providence and destiny lay the conviction of the progressive march of civilization that was characteristic of eighteenth- and nineteenth-century views about the nature of the historical process. If he conceded some important aspects of civilization to the Mexicans, not least in 'astronomical science', which he described as being 'so disproportioned to their progress in other walks of civilization'[15], he noted as indicators of their lack of civility their 'bigotry' and 'superstition', and the 'revolting usages'[16] of their priests, including human sacrifice. In this, Montezuma was a faithful representative of the Aztec people, as Prescott makes plain in his verdict on the emperor: 'If we cannot refuse our contempt for the pusillanimity of the Aztec monarch, it should be mitigated by the consideration, that his pusillanimity sprung from his superstition, and that superstition in the savage is the substitute for religious principle in the civilised man.'[17] All the more curious, then, that Montezuma's equally superstitious subjects should have displayed such courage and endurance as they fought to save Tenochtitlan.

In writing of Aztec superstition – exemplified by the faith placed by Montezuma in oracles and prophecies, and his supposed identification of Cortés with the returning god Quetzalcoatl[18] – Prescott was confronted by something of a dilemma. In the eyes of nineteenth-century Anglo–Americans, Spanish civilization was itself a byword for bigotry and superstition. It was the Protestant world, not the Catholic, that was in the vanguard of human progress, and the image of Spain was indelibly tarnished by the Black Legend of Spanish cruelty and fanaticism.[19] Prescott, as a historian of Spain who was also a convinced Protestant, naturally had to face up in his work to the question of Spanish religion. He confronted it head-on in the pen-portrait of Cortés with which the *Conquest* concludes: 'One trait more remains to be noticed in the character of this remarkable man: that is, his bigotry, the failing of the age, – for, surely, it should be termed only a failing... We should throw ourselves back (it cannot be too often repeated) into the age; the age of the Crusades. For every Spanish cavalier, however sordid and selfish might be his private motives, felt himself to be the soldier of the Cross... To the more rational spirit of the present day, it may seem difficult to reconcile gross deviations from morals with such devotion to the cause of religion. But the religion taught in that day was one of form and elaborate ceremony... In a worship that is addressed too exclusively to the senses, it is often the case that morality becomes divorced from religion...'[20] In other words, Cortés and his fellow Spaniards were motivated by true religion, even if in that religion, in its Roman Catholic version, could now be seen as defective. No such concession was made to the superstitious Montezuma and his fellow Aztecs.

The scales were thus tilted against the Aztecs from the start, and continued to be so as the drama unfolded. While Prescott allowed the Aztecs, with the exception of their emperor, to be highly courageous, as befitted a people still not far removed from savagery, he was inclined to attribute to their methods of warfare such characteristics as deceit, duplicity and treachery, while glossing over the fact that the Spaniards could be tarred with just the same brush.[21] Cortés is all too often accorded the benefit of the doubt, as in the fateful decision to take Montezuma into custody. Prescott expresses his own doubts about the morality of the 'kidnapping of a friendly sovereign', but then goes on to argue that 'to view the matter differently, we must take the position of the Conquerors, and assume with them the original right of conquest. Regarded from this point of view, many difficulties vanish. If conquest were a duty, whatever was necessary to effect it was right also. Right and expedient become convertible terms...'[22] Explaining can all too easily drift into explaining away.

Prescott was inevitably largely dependent on his Spanish sources, in particular Cortés's own 'Letters of Relation'[23] and Bernal Díaz's wonderful eyewitness chronicle of the conquest.[24] But while well aware of the need to scrutinize these sources carefully, he also needed, for the purposes of his drama, to present Cortés as endowed with the qualities of the hero. 'Cortés', he writes, 'was not a vulgar conqueror.' Rather, 'he was a knight-errant, in the literal sense of the word.'[25] The story of the conquest of Mexico for Prescott is the story of the triumph of bold ambition, and of astute and intelligent leadership that amounted to genius. Cortés, like a true knight-errant, set forth on a mission that lesser men would have regarded as impossible, but by sheer courage and force of personality he vanquished all the odds. He was seen at his greatest at the moment of disaster, the *noche triste* of his forced retreat from Tenochtitlan: 'Circumstances so appalling as would have paralysed a common mind, only stimulated his to higher action, and drew forth all its resources. He combined what is most rare, singular coolness and constancy of purpose, with a spirit of enterprise that might well be called romantic.'[26]

By concentrating attention on Cortés and his qualities as a leader, Prescott was able to give the story of the conquest a dramatic unity. He does not neglect the band of men under Cortés's command, men who 'bore hearts stout and courageous as ever beat in human bosoms'[27], nor does he ignore the part played by Cortés's Indian allies in his ultimate success, but over and over again at the moments of crisis it is Cortés who saves the day through his bravery and resourcefulness. This gives the seven books of *The Conquest of Mexico* an architectural unity that was one of the reasons for its success. Inevitably a feeling for the structure of the narrative is lost when it is not read in its entirety, but something of it can be glimpsed from the selections from books 3 to 5 included in this volume, most notably the episode of Cortés's defeat of the expedition sent to overthrow him under the command of the perfect anti-hero, the lax and arrogant Pánfilo de Narváez, and the searing account of the retreat from Tenochtitlan. At that point the Spaniards appeared to have lost everything, but in the book which follows, and which is not included here, the indomitable Cortés again rises to the occasion, lays siege to the Aztec capital, and finally ensures the overthrow of the Aztec empire and the conquest of Mexico for Spain.

In both these episodes Prescott's narrative style is displayed at its best, so perfectly paced that even today's readers, conditioned by fast-paced drama and powerful visual imagery, are still likely to be gripped by the excitement of the story. Inevitably, here as elsewhere, Victorian turns of phrase tend at times to make his prose appear overblown, just as it can also lapse into the stately. In some respects, indeed, *The Conquest of Mexico* is not unlike a Victorian pageant, with one tableau succeeding another against an exotic backdrop. Cortés's army, for instance, is described as descending towards 'the broad plains of the *tierra caliente*, spread out like a boundless ocean of verdure below them.'[28] It is another perfect tableau. Even if Prescott's forests have a tendency to be 'verdant' rather than green, he can summon up sights and sounds in ways that still resonate with a modern reader. For all the occasional grandiloquence of his style, he remains a master both of the formal set-piece and of dramatic movement.

Inevitably, in style and conception *The Conquest of Mexico* remains very much of its age, and this has naturally diminished its usefulness as a historical source as the years have passed. The Spanish texts on which Prescott was dependent remain as fundamental to the story in our day as in his, but are nowadays read with a rather more critical eye than that with which he tended to appraise them. His idealization of Cortés as the quintessential hero prevented him from appreciating the complexity of his character, and made him a one-dimensional figure. It is now generally appreciated that Cortés's letters are self-serving documents that cannot be taken at their face value, and sometimes come closer to fiction than to historical fact.[29] Full of admiration for his hero, Prescott was inclined to dismiss criticisms of Cortés as mere slanders by his enemies, but extensive use of the documents produced during the course of the judicial inquiry into his activities and preserved in Seville's Archive of the Indies, has made possible the more nuanced portrait presented in Hugh Thomas's *The Conquest of Mexico*, the closest modern approximation to Prescott's grand narrative.[30]

It is, however, on the Mexican rather than the Spanish side of the story that the picture painted by Prescott has been most dramatically transformed. The reasons for this are various. Archaeology has transformed our knowledge of pre-conquest Mexico. Intensive work has been done on the interpretation of Mexican pictographs[31], and on the texts of indigenous Nahuatl accounts of the conquest.[32] Above all, a profound change in Western attitudes towards the non-Western world occurred in the course of the twentieth century, as colonial empires collapsed and former colonial peoples began to claim their places in the sun. With these changes, the condescending view of non-Western civilizations that informed the approach of Prescott and his contemporaries lost its hold, and it became deeply unfashionable to see history as the story of the slow but steady progress of the human race towards the level of 'civilization' achieved by the West. As part of this process of re-evaluation, historians set out to recover 'the vision of the vanquished'[33], and to reconstruct the histories of 'peoples without history'[34], victims not only of imperial domination but also of the lack of written records.

The Aztecs have been among the beneficiaries of this process, and in recent years ethnographers and historians have made ambitious efforts to see their civilization in its own terms, rather than filtered through the distorting lens held up by their conquerors.[35] The same holds true of the history of the conquest itself, as historians try to tease out an indigenous version of events from contemporary or near-contemporary indigenous accounts, many of them collected by the Spanish friar Bernardino de Sahagún and preserved in Book XII of the *Florentine Codex*.[36] But while a sympathetic reading of these and other sources may have brought us closer than Prescott to an understanding of indigenous perceptions of the conquest, the whole exercise remains problematic. How far can we rely on the memories of people trying to make sense of what had happened two or three decades after the event, and many of them still traumatized by the collapse of the world they had known or dimly remembered? Even where the oral tradition remained unbroken and memories were reasonably accurate, can we be sure that these Christian converts transmitted the information in unvarnished form to the friars who recorded their words, rather than conforming it to the expectations of their religious mentors? Equally, how far did the friars themselves really understand and accurately record what their Nahua informants were telling them?

These and similar questions about the reliability of the available evidence have bedevilled all attempts, from Prescott's time to our own, to solve some of the difficult problems that face every historian or would-be historian of the conquest. Prescott, for instance, found in the account of the omens preceding the arrival of the Spaniards, and also in the story of the expected return of Quetzalcoatl to reclaim the land from which he had long ago been driven, an explanation of Montezuma's strange passivity in the face of Cortés and his men: 'He felt as if the destinies which had so long brooded over the royal line of Mexico were to be accomplished, and the sceptre was to pass away from his house for ever.'[37] Montezuma's assumed identification of Cortés with Quetzalcoatl has been a staple element of the story from Prescott's day to our own, but it has also come to be contested as a post-conquest fabrication.[38] Equally, the omens have been shown to possess suspicious affinities with the omens and prodigies recorded by classical authors like Plutarch, Lucan and Josephus.[39] If the Quetzalcoatl myth and the story of the omens are no more than retrospective attempts to make sense of the extraordinary succession of events, Prescott's doom-laden interpretation of Montezuma's behaviour loses much of its credibility.

In spite of the advance of knowledge about the belief systems of the Aztecs and their cyclical concept of history, it seems unlikely that the mystery of the Quetzalcoatl story will ever be solved. The evidence is simply too thin. The same remains true of another of the great mysteries of the conquest: the true cause of Montezuma's death. Was he killed by stones thrown by his own rebellious subjects, as the account commonly goes, or was he put to death by the Spaniards, as one or two alternative sources suggest? Or did he perhaps die 'as much under the anguish of a wounded spirit, as under disease', as Prescott was inclined to believe?[40] Again it is highly improbable that the truth will ever be known.

Although Prescott was well aware of the problems of evidence, the history of the conquest of Mexico remains far more complex than he imagined it. For him, it was the story of the overthrow of an empire that was doomed to defeat by the superiority, spiritual as well as material, of the European civilization that brought about its downfall. He could look on the defeated with admiration for their bravery and with a real sense of compassion, but the comment in his Literary Memoranda as he wrote up the *noche triste* tells its own story: 'It did not cost me as much to kill Montezuma – as it did Isabella, tho' I rather love the barbarian.'[41] The future belonged to the white races of the north, and the moral and spiritual inferiority of the Aztecs inevitably consigned them to the dust-heap of history.

Yet, for all its limitations, Prescott's *History of the Conquest of Mexico* still casts its spell. He may have made his mistakes, but he sifted the evidence carefully, and much of his narrative has stood the test of time. Although he idealized Cortés, he appreciated, as some of his successors have not, that the conquest of Mexico was not simply a foreign conquest, but also a Mexican civil war. 'The Aztec monarchy', he wrote, 'fell by the hands of its own subjects, under the direction of European sagacity and science.'[42] Later historians have naturally brought further evidence into play, and in particular have achieved a greater understanding of the civilization that was overthrown between 1519 and 1521. But they have not come much nearer to solving the mysteries that baffled Prescott; and, while necessarily complicating the story in their pursuit of a closer approximation to the truth, they have deprived it of something of the epic character with which he endowed it. When it came to providing a narrative of Cortés's conquest of Mexico the very weaknesses of Prescott – his idealization of the self-reliant individual, his Bostonian assumptions and prejudices, his predilection for vivid romance – turned out to be his greatest source of strength. By reducing the story to an epic drama with poetic and melancholy overtones, he made it unforgettable for generations of readers.

J.H. Elliott

SUGGESTIONS FOR FURTHER READING

Clendinnen, Inga, *Aztecs* (Cambridge: Cambridge University Press, 1991).

Cortés, Hernán, *Letters from Mexico*, trans. and ed. Antony Pagden (New Haven and London: Yale University Press, 1986).

Díaz, Bernal, *The Conquest of New Spain*, trans. J. M. Cohen (Harmondsworth: Penguin Books, 1963).

Hassig, Ross, *Mexico and the Spanish Conquest* (London and New York: Longman, 1994).

Leon-Portilla, Miguel (ed.), *The Broken Spears: The Aztec Account of the Conquest of Mexico* (Boston: Beacon Press, 1962; London: Constable, 1962).

Thomas, Hugh, *The Conquest of Mexico* (London: Hutchinson, 1993).

NOTES

1. Cited in R. A. Humphreys, *William Hickling Prescott: The Man and the Historian* (*Diamante* IX, London: The Hispanic and Luso-Brazilian Councils, 1959), p. 26.

2. Prescott's life was written by his friend, the literary scholar, George Ticknor, *Life of William Hickling Prescott* (Boston: Ticknor and Fields, 1864; repr. London, 1904).

3. Ticknor, *Life of Prescott* (1904), pp. 95–6.

4. C. Harvey Gardiner (ed.), *The Literary Memoranda of William Hickling Prescott* (2 vols, Norman, Oklahoma: University of Oklahoma Press, 1961), i, p.55.

5. *Literary Memoranda*, i, pp. 227–30 (27 May 1838).

6. For a collective study of the nineteenth-century Boston historians, see David Levin, *History as Romantic Art: Bancroft, Prescott, Motley and Parkman* (Stanford, California: Stanford University Press, 1959).

7. Levin, *History as Romantic Art*, p.11.

8. For 'philosophic history', see John Burrow, *A History of Histories* (London: Allen Lane, 2007), ch. 21.

9. *Literary Memoranda*, ii, p. 13.

10. *Literary Memoranda*, ii, p. 69.

11. *Literary Memoranda*, ii, p. 32.

12. W. H. Prescott, *The Conquest of Mexico* (2 vols, London: Everyman edn, 1957), i, p. 348 (below, p. 41).

13. *Conquest*, ii, p. 49 (below, p. 108).

14. *Conquest*, i, p. 377.

15. *Conquest*, i, p. 81.

16. *Conquest*, i, p. 56.

17. *Conquest*, ii, pp. 88–9

18. *Conquest*, i, pp. 42–3

19. For Prescott's contribution to the image, see Richard L. Kagan, 'Prescott's Paradigm: American Historical Scholarship and the Decline of Spain', *American Historical Review*, 101 (1996), pp. 423–46, reprinted as an appendix to Richard L. Kagan (ed.), *Spain in America. The Origins of Hispanism in the United States* (Urbana and Chicago: University of Illinois Press, 2002).

20. *Conquest*, ii, pp. 367–8.

21. Levin, *History as a Romantic Art*, p. 155.

22. *Conquest*, i, p. 397.

23. Hernán Cortés, *Letters from Mexico* (trans. and ed. Antony Pagden, New Haven and London: Yale University Press, 1971; revised edn 1986).

24. Bernal Díaz, *The Conquest of New Spain* (trans. J. M. Cohen, Harmondsworth: Penguin Books, 1963).

25. *Conquest*, ii, pp. 365 and 362.

26. *Conquest*, ii, pp. 79–80 (below, p. 125).

27. *Conquest*, ii, p. 30 (below, p. 93).

28. *Conquest*, ii, p. 30 (below, p. 94).

29. See, for example, Anthony Pagden's edition of Cortés's *Letters from Mexico*, and 'The Mental World of Hernán Cortés' in J. H. Elliott, *Spain and its World, 1500–1700* (New Haven and London: Yale University Press, 1989), ch. 2.

30. (London: Hutchinson, 1993).

31. For an attractive sampling, see Serge Gruzinski, *Painting the Conquest: The Mexican Indians and the European Renaissance* (Paris: Flammarion, 1992).

32. See, for example, Miguel Leon-Portilla (ed.), T*he Broken Spears: The Aztec Account of the Conquest of Mexico* (Boston: Beacon Press, 1962; London: Constable, 1962); *We People Here: Nahuatl Accounts of the Conquest of Mexico*, trans. and ed. James Lockhart (Berkeley, Los Angeles, London: UCLA Center for Medieval and Renaissance Studies, 1993).

33. The title of the original Spanish version (1959) of Leon-Portilla's *Broken Spears*.

34. Eric R. Wolf, *Europe and the People Without History* (Berkeley, Los Angeles, London: UCLA Center for Medieval and Renaissance Studies, 1982).

35. See, for example, the vivid account by Inga Clendinnen, *Aztecs* (Cambridge: Cambridge University Press, 1991).

36. For translations into English of the Nahuatl and Spanish texts see Lockhart (ed.), *We People Here*, pp. 48–255.

37. *Conquest*, i, pp. 194–6.

38. For a questioning of the Quetzalcoatl thesis, see Elliott, 'The Mental World of Hernán Cortés', and Susan D. Gillespie, *The Aztec Kings: the Construction of Rulership in Mexican History* (Tucson, Arizona: University of Arizona Press, 1989), ch. 6.

39. Felipe Fernández-Armesto, '"Aztec"Auguries and Memories of the Conquest of Mexico', *Renaissance Studies*, 6 (1992), pp. 287–305.

40. *Conquest*, ii, p. 85 (below, p. 131).

41. *Literary Memoranda*, ii, p. 90 (11 July 1842).

42. *Conquest*, ii, pp. 286–7

HISTORY OF THE
CONQUEST OF MEXICO

In 1518, Hernando Cortés had persuaded Diego de Velázquez, governor of Cuba, to make him commander of an expedition to Mexico. Shortly before Cortés set sail, Velázquez, who was now suspicious of his motives, had cancelled his commission, but Cortés had ignored Velázquez and had set out none the less, sailing up the Yucatan coast. Soon after his arrival in Mexico, Cortés renounced the authority of Velázquez, and decided to rely exclusively on the support of the crown in Spain. In August 1519, Cortés and his army reached Tlaxcala, a Nahua city, where, after weeks of negotiation, the Spaniards sealed an alliance with the Tlaxcalans. Soon afterwards, Cortés headed for the city of Cholula. The major civilization in the region, however, was that of the Aztecs, led by Montezuma II. After a three-month journey over difficult terrain, Cortés arrived in the Aztec capital, Tenochtitlan, in November 1519.

With the first faint streak of dawn, the Spanish general was up, mustering his followers. They gathered, with beating hearts, under their respective banners as the trumpet sent forth its spirit-stirring sounds across water and woodland, till they died away in distant echoes among the mountains. The sacred flames on the altars of numberless *teocallis*, dimly seen through the grey mists of morning, indicated the site of the capital, till temple, tower, and palace were fully revealed in the glorious illumination which the sun, as he rose above the eastern barrier, poured over the beautiful valley. It was the eight of November, 1519; a conspicuous day in history, as that on which the Europeans first set foot in the capital of the Western World.

Cortés with his little body of horse formed a sort of advanced guard to the army. Then came the Spanish infantry, who in a summer's campaign had acquired the discipline, and the weather-beaten aspect, of veterans. The baggage occupied the centre; and the rear was closed by the dark files of Tlascalan warriors. The whole number must have fallen short of seven thousand; of which less than four hundred were Spaniards.

For a short distance, the army kept along the narrow tongue of land that divides the Tezcucan from the Chalcan waters, when it entered on the great dike which, with the exception of an angle near the commencement, stretches in a perfectly straight line across the salt floods of Tezcuco to the gates of the capital. It was the same causeway, or rather the basis of that, which still forms the great southern avenue of Mexico. The Spaniards had occasion more than ever to admire the mechanical science of the Aztecs, in the geometrical precision with which the work was executed, as well as the solidity of its construction. It was composed of huge stones well laid in cement; and wide enough, throughout its whole extent, for ten horsemen to ride abreast.

They saw, as they passed along, several large towns, resting on piles, and reaching far into the water, – a kind of architecture which found great favour with the Aztecs, being in imitation of that of their metropolis. The busy population obtained a good subsistence from the manufacture of salt, which they extracted from the waters of the great lake. The duties on the traffic in this article were a considerable source of revenue to the crown.

Everywhere the Conquerors beheld the evidence of a crowded and thriving population, exceeding all they had yet seen. The temples and principal buildings of the cities were covered with a hard white stucco, which glistened like enamel in the level beams of the morning. The margin of the great basin was more thickly gemmed, than that of Chalco, with towns and hamlets. The water was darkened by swarms of canoes filled with Indians, who clambered up the sides of the causeway, and gazed with curious astonishment on the strangers. And here, also, they beheld those fairy islands of flowers, overshadowed occasionally by trees of considerable size, rising and falling with the gentle undulation of the billows. At the distance of half a league from the capital, they encountered a solid work or curtain of stone, which traversed the dike. It was twelve feet high, was strengthened by towers at the extremities, and in the centre was a battlemented gate-way, which opened a passage to the troops. It was called the Fort of Xoloc, and became memorable in after times as the position occupied by Cortés in the famous siege of Mexico.

Here they were met by several hundred Aztec chiefs, who came out to announce the approach of Montezuma, and to welcome the Spaniards to his capital. They were dressed in the fanciful gala costume of the country, with the *maxtlatl*, or cotton sash, around their loins and a broad mantle of the same material, or of the brilliant feather-embroidery, flowing gracefully down their shoulders. On their necks and arms they displayed collars and bracelets of turquoise mosaic, with which delicate plumage was curiously mingled, while their ears, under-lips, and occasionally their noses, were garnished with pendants formed of precious stones, or crescents of fine gold. As each cacique made the usual formal salutation of the country separately to the general, the tedious ceremony delayed the march more than an hour. After this, the army experienced no further interruption till it reached a bridge near the gates of the city. It was built of wood, since replaced by one of stone, and was thrown across an opening of the dike, which furnished an outlet to the waters, when agitated by the winds, or swollen by a sudden influx in the rainy season. It was a draw-bridge; and the Spaniards, as they crossed it, felt how truly they were committing themselves to the mercy of Montezuma, who, by thus cutting off their communications with the country, might hold them prisoners in his capital.

In the midst of these unpleasant reflections, they beheld the glittering retinue of the emperor emerging from the great street which led then, as it still does, through the heart of the city. Amidst a crowd of Indian nobles, preceded by three officers of state, bearing golden wands, they saw the royal palanquin blazing with burnished gold. It was borne on the shoulders of nobles, and over it a canopy of gaudy feather-work, powdered with jewels, and fringed with silver, was supported by four attendants of the same rank. They were bare-footed, and walked with a slow, measured pace, and with eyes bent on the ground. When the train had come within a convenient distance, it halted, and Montezuma, descending from his litter, came forward leaning on the arms of the lords of Tezcuco and Iztapalapan, his nephew and brother, both of whom, as we have seen, had already been made known to the Spaniards. As the monarch advanced under the canopy, the obsequious attendants strewed the ground with cotton tapestry, that his imperial feet might not be contaminated by the rude soil. His subjects of high and low degree, who lined the sides of the causeway, bent forward with their eyes fastened on the ground as he passed, and some of the humbler class prostrated themselves before him. Such was the homage paid to the Indian despot, showing that the slavish forms of Oriental adulation were to be found among the rude inhabitants of the Western World.

Montezuma wore the girdle and ample square cloak, *tilmatli*, of his nation. It was made of the finest cotton, with the embroidered ends gathered in a knot round his neck. His feet were defended by sandals having soles of gold, and the leathern thongs which bound them to his ankles were embossed with the same metal. Both the cloak and sandals were sprinkled with pearls and precious stones, among which the emerald and the *chalchivitl* – a green stone of higher estimation than any other among the Aztecs – were conspicuous. On his head he wore no other ornament than a *panache* of plumes of the royal green which floated down his back, the badge of military rather than of regal rank.

He was at this time about forty years of age. His person was tall and thin, but not ill-made. His hair, which was black and straight, was not very long; to wear it short was considered unbecoming persons of rank. His beard was thin; his complexion somewhat paler than is often found in his dusky, or rather copper-colored race. His features, though serious in their expression, did not wear the look of melancholy, indeed, of dejection, which characterizes his portrait, and which may well have settled on them at a later period. He moved with dignity, and his whole demeanour, tempered by an expression of benignity not to have been anticipated from the reports circulated of his character, was worthy of a great prince. – Such is the portrait left to us of the celebrated Indian emperor, in this his first interview with the white men.

The army halted as he drew near. Cortés, dismounting, threw his reins to a page, and, supported by a few of the principal cavaliers, advanced to meet him. The interview must have been one of uncommon interest to both. In Montezuma, Cortés beheld the lord of the broad realms he had traversed, whose magnificence and power had been the burden of every tongue. In the Spaniard, on the other hand, the Aztec prince saw the strange being whose history seemed to be so mysteriously connected with his own; the predicted one of his oracles; whose achievements proclaimed him something more than human. But, whatever may have been the monarch's feelings, he so far suppressed them as to receive his guest with princely courtesy, and to express his satisfaction at personally seeing him in his capital. Cortés responded by the most profound expressions of respect, while he made ample acknowledgements for the substantial proofs which the emperor had given the Spaniards of his munificence. He then hung round Montezuma's neck a sparkling chain of colored crystal, accompanying this with a movement as if to embrace him, when he was restrained by the two Aztec lords, shocked at the menaced profanation of the sacred person of their master. After the interchange of these civilities, Montezuma appointed his brother to conduct the Spaniards to their residence in the capital, and again entering his litter, was borne off amidst prostrate crowds in the same state in which he had come. The Spaniards quickly followed, and with colors flying and music playing, soon made their entrance into the southern quarter of Tenochtitlan.

Here, again, they found fresh cause for admiration in the grandeur of the city, and the superior style of its architecture. The dwellings of the poorer class were, indeed, chiefly of reeds and mud. But the great avenue through which they were now arching was lined with the houses of the nobles, who were encouraged by the emperor to make the capital their residence. They were built of a red porous stone drawn from quarries in the neighbourhood, and, though they rarely rose to a second story, often covered a large space of ground. The flat roofs, *azoteas*, were protected by stone parapets, so that every house was a fortress. Sometimes these roofs resembled parterres of flowers, so thickly they were covered with them, but more frequently these were cultivated in broad terraced gardens, laid out between the edifices. Occasionally a great square or market-place intervened, surrounded by its porticoes of stone and stucco; or a pyramidal temple reared its colossal bulk, crowned with its tapering sanctuaries, and altars blazing with inextinguishable fires. The great street facing the southern causeway, unlike most others in the place, was wide, and extended some miles in nearly a straight line, as before noticed, through the centre of the city. A spectator standing at one end of it, as his eye ranged along the deep vista of temples, terraces, and gardens, might clearly discern the other, with the blue mountains in the distances, which, in the transparent atmosphere of the table-land, seemed almost in contact with the buildings.

But what most impressed the Spaniards was the throng of people who swarmed through the streets and on the canals, filling every door-way and window, and clustering on the roofs of the buildings. "I well remember the spectacle," exclaims Bernal Diaz; "it seems now, after so many years, as present to my mind as if it were but yesterday." But what must have been the sensations of the Aztecs themselves, as they looked on the portentous pageant! as they heard, now for the first time, the well-cemented pavement ring under the iron tramp of the horses, – the strange animals which fear had clothed in such supernatural terrors; as they gazed on the children of the East, revealing their celestial origin in their fair complexions; saw the bright falchions and bonnets of steel, a metal to them unknown, glancing like meteors in the sun, while sounds of unearthly music – at least, such as their rude instruments had never wakened – floated in the air! But every other emotion was lost in that of deadly hatred, when they beheld their detested enemy, the Tlascalan, stalking, in defiance, as it were, through their streets, and staring around with looks of ferocity and wonder, like some wild animal of the forest, who had strayed by chance from his native fastnesses into the haunts of civilization.

As they passed down the spacious street, the troops repeatedly traversed bridges suspended above canals, along which they saw the Indian barks gliding swiftly with their little cargoes of fruits and vegetables for the markets of Tenochtitlan. At length, they halted before a broad area near the centre of the city, where rose the huge pyramidal pile dedicated to the patron war-god of the Aztecs, second only, in size, as well as sanctity, to the temple of Cholula, and covering the same ground now in part occupied by the great cathedral of Mexico.

Facing the western gate of the inclosure of the temple, stood a low range of stone buildings, spreading over a wide extent of ground, the palace of Axayacatl, Montezuma's father, built by that monarch about fifty years before. It was appropriated as the barracks of the Spaniards. The emperor himself was in the courtyard, waiting to receive them. Approaching Cortés, he took from a vase of flowers, borne by one of his slaves, a massy collar, in which the shell of a species of craw-fish, much prized by the Indians, was set in gold, and connected by heavy links of the same metal. From this chain depended eight ornaments, also of gold, make in resemblance of the same shell-fish, a span in length each, and of delicate workmanship; for the Aztec goldsmiths were confessed to have shown skill in their craft, not inferior to their brethren of Europe. Montezuma, as he hung the gorgeous collar round the general's neck, said, "This palace belongs to you, Malinche," (the epithet by which he always addressed him,) "and your brethren. Rest after your fatigues, for you have much need to do so, and in a little while I will visit you again." So saying, he withdrew with his attendants, evincing, in this act, a deliberate consideration not to have been expected in a barbarian.

Cortés first care was to inspect his new quarters. The building, though spacious, was low, consisting of one floor, except, indeed, in the centre, where it rose to an additional story. The apartments were of great size, and afforded accommodations, according to the testimony of the Conquerors themselves, for the whole army! The hardy mountaineers of Tlascala were, probably, not very fastidious, and might easily find a shelter in the out-buildings, or under temporary awnings in the ample court-yards. The best apartments were hung with gay cotton draperies, the floors covered with mats or rushes. There were, also, low stools made of single pieces of wood elaborately carved, and in most of the apartments beds made of the palm-leaf, woven into a thick mat, with coverlets, and sometimes canopies of cotton. These mats were the only beds used by the natives, whether of high or low degree.

After a rapid survey of this gigantic pile, the general assigned his troops their respective quarters, and took as vigilant precautions for security, as if he had anticipated a siege, instead of a friendly entertainment. The place was encompassed by a stone wall of considerable thickness, with towers or heavy buttresses at intervals, affording a good means of defence. He planted his cannon so as to command the approaches, stationed his sentinels along the works, and, in short, enforced in every respect as strict military discipline as had been observed in any part of the march. He well knew the importance to his little band, at least, for the present, of conciliating the good-will of the citizens; and, to avoid all possibility of collision, he prohibited any soldier from leaving his quarters without orders, under pain of death. Having taken these precautions, he allowed his men to partake of the bountiful collation which had been prepared for them.

They had been long enough in the country to become reconciled to, if not to relish, the peculiar cooking of the Aztecs. The appetite of the soldier is not often dainty, and on the present occasion it cannot be doubted that the Spaniards did full justice to the savory productions of the royal kitchen. During the meal they were served by numerous Mexican slaves, who were, indeed, distributed through the palace, anxious to do the bidding of the strangers. After the repast was concluded, and they had taken their *siesta*, not less important to a Spaniard than food itself, the presence of the emperor was again announced.

36

Montezuma was attended by a few of his principal nobles. He was received with much deference by Cortés; and, after the parties had taken their seats, a conversation commenced between them through the aid of Doña Marina, while the cavaliers and Aztec chieftains stood around in respectful silence.

Montezuma made many inquiries concerning the country of the Spaniards, their sovereign, the nature of his government, and especially their own motives in visiting Anahuac. Cortés explained these motives by the desire to see so distinguished a monarch, and to declare to him the true Faith professed by the Christians. With rare discretion, he contented himself with dropping this hint, for the present allowing it to ripen in the mind of the emperor, till a future conference. The latter asked, whether those white men, who in the preceding year had landed on the eastern shores of his empire, were their countrymen. He showed himself well informed of the proceedings of the Spaniards from their arrival in Tabasco to the present time, information of which had been regularly transmitted in the hieroglyphical paintings. He was curious, also, in regard to the rank of his visitors in their own country; inquiring, if they were the kinsmen of the sovereign. Cortés replied, they were kinsmen of one another, and subjects of their great monarch, who held them all in peculiar estimation. Before his departure, Montezuma made himself acquainted with the names of the principal cavaliers, and the position they occupied in the army.

At the conclusion of the interview, the Aztec prince commanded his attendants to bring forward the presents prepared for his guests. They consisted of cotton dresses, enough to supply every man, it is said, including the allies, with a suit! And he did not fail to add the usual accompaniment of gold chains and other ornaments, which he distributed in profusion among the Spaniards. He then withdrew with the same ceremony with which he had entered, leaving every one deeply impressed with his munificence, and his affability, so unlike what they had been taught to expect, by, what they now considered, an invention of the enemy.

That evening, the Spaniards celebrated their arrival in the Mexican capital by a general discharge of artillery. The thunders of the ordnance reverberating among the buildings and shaking them to their foundations, the stench of the sulphureous vapor that rolled in volumes above the walls of the encampment, reminding the inhabitants of the explosions of the great *volcan*, filled the hearts of the superstitious Aztecs with dismay. It proclaimed to them, that their city held in its bosom those dread beings whose path had been marked with desolation, and who could call down the thunderbolts to consume their enemies! It was doubtless the policy of Cortés to strengthen this superstitious feeling as far as possible, and to impress the natives, at the outset, with a salutary awe of the supernatural powers of the Spaniards.

On the following morning, the general requested permission to return the emperor's visit, by waiting on him in his palace. This was readily granted, and Montezuma sent his officers to conduct the Spaniards to his presence. Cortés dressed himself in his richest habit, and left the quarters attended by Alvarado, Sandoval, Velasquez, and Ordaz, together with five or six of the common file.

The royal habitation was at no great distance. It stood on the ground, to the south-west of the cathedral, since covered in part by the *casa del Estado*, the palace of the dukes of Monteleone, the descendants of Cortés. It was a vast, irregular pile of low stone buildings, like that garrisoned by the Spaniards. So spacious was it, indeed, that, as one of the Conquerors assures us, although he had visited it more than once, for the express purpose, he had been too much fatigued each time by wandering through the apartments ever to see the whole of it. It was built of the red porous stone of the country, *tetzontli*, was ornamented with marble, and on the façade over the principal entrance were sculptured the arms or device of Montezuma, an eagle bearing an ocelot in his talons.

In the courts through which the Spaniards passed, fountains of crystal water were playing, fed from the copious reservoir on the distant hill of Chapoltepec, and supplying in their turn more than a hundred baths in the interior of the palace. Crowds of Aztec nobles were sauntering up and down in these squares, and in the outer halls, loitering away their hours in attendance on the court. The apartments were of immense size, though not lofty. The ceilings were of various sorts of odoriferous wood ingeniously carved; the floors covered with mats of the palm-leaf. The walls were hung with cotton richly stained, with the skins of wild animals, or gorgeous draperies of feather-work wrought in imitation of birds, insects, and flowers, with the nice art and glowing radiance of colours that might compare with the tapestries of Flanders. Clouds of incense rolled up from censers, and diffused intoxicating odors through the apartments. The Spaniards might well have fancied themselves in the voluptuous precincts of an Eastern harem, instead of treading the halls of a wild barbaric chief in the Western World.

On reaching the hall of audience, the Mexican officers took off their sandals, and covered their gay attire with a mantle of *nequen*, a coarse stuff made of the fibres of the maguey, worn only by the poorest classes. This act of humiliation was imposed on all, except the members of his own family, who approached the sovereign. Thus bare-footed, with down-case eyes, and formal obeisance, they ushered the Spaniards into the royal presence.

They found Montezuma seated at the further end of a spacious saloon, and surrounded by a few of his favorite chiefs. He received them kindly, and very soon Cortés, without much ceremony, entered on the subject which was uppermost in his thoughts. He was fully aware of the importance of gaining the royal convert, whose example would have such an influence on the conversion of his people. The general, therefore, prepared to display the whole store of his theological science, with the most winning arts of rhetoric he could command, while the interpretation was conveyed through the silver tones of Marina, as inseparable from him, on these occasions, as his shadow.

He set forth, as clearly as he could, the ideas entertained by the Church in regard to the holy mysteries of the Trinity, the Incarnation, and the Atonement. From this he ascended to the origin of things, the creation of the world, the first pair, paradise, and the fall of man. He assured Montezuma, that the idols he worshipped were Satan under different forms. A sufficient proof of it was the bloody sacrifices they imposed, which he contrasted with the pure and simple rite of the mass. Their worship would sink him in perdition. It was to snatch his soul, and the souls of his people, from the flames of eternal fire by opening to them a purer faith, that the Christians had come to his land. And he earnestly besought him not to neglect the occasion, but to secure his salvation by embracing the Cross, the greatest sign of human redemption.

The eloquence of the preacher was wasted on the insensible heart of his royal auditor. It, doubtless, lost somewhat of its efficacy, strained through the imperfect interpretation of so recent a neophyte as the Indian damsel. But the doctrines were too abstruse in themselves to be comprehended at a glance by the rude intellect of a barbarian. And Montezuma may have, perhaps, thought it was not more monstrous to feed on the flesh of a fellow-creature, than on that of the Creator himself. He was, besides, steeped in the superstitions of his country from his cradle. He had been educated in the straightest sect of her religion; had been himself a priest before his election to the throne; and was now the head both of the religion and the state. Little probability was there that such a man would be open to argument or persuasion, even from the lips of a more practised polemic than the Spanish commander. How could he abjure the faith that was intertwined with the dearest affections of his heart, and the very elements of his being? How could he be false to the gods who had raised him to such prosperity and honors, and whose shrines were intrusted to his especial keeping?

He listened, however, with silent attention, until the general had concluded his homily. He then replied, that he knew the Spaniards had held this discourse wherever they had been. He doubted not their God was, as they said, a good being. His gods, also, were good to him. Yet what his visitor said of the creation of the world was like what he had been taught to believe. It was not worth while to discourse

41

further of the matter. His ancestors, he said, were not the original proprietors of the land. They had occupied it but a few ages, and had been led there by a great Being, who, after giving them laws and ruling over the nation for a time, had withdrawn to the regions where the sun rises. He had declared, on his departure, that he or his descendents would again visit them and resume his empire. The wonderful deeds of the Spaniards, their fair complexions, and the quarter whence they came, all showed they were his descendants. If Montezuma had resisted their visit to his capital it was because he had heard such accounts of their cruelties, – that they sent the lightning to consume his people, or crushed them to pieces under the hard feet of the ferocious animals on which they rode. He was now convinced that these were idle tales; that the Spaniards were kind and generous in their natures; they were mortals of a different race, indeed, from the Aztecs, wiser, and more valiant, – and for this he honored them.

"You, too" he added, with a smile, "have been told, perhaps, that I am a god, and dwell in palaces of gold and silver. But you see it is false. My houses, though large, are of stone and wood like those of others; and as to my body," he said, baring his tawny arm, "you see it is flesh and bone like yours. It is true, I have a great empire, inherited from my ancestors; lands, and gold, and silver. But your sovereign beyond the waters is, I know, the rightful lord of all. I rule in his name. You, Malintzin, are his ambassador; you and your brethren shall share these things with me. Rest now from your labors. You are here in your own dwellings, and every thing shall be provided for your subsistence. I will see that your wishes shall be obeyed in the same way as my own."

As the monarch concluded these words, a few natural tears suffused his eyes, while the image of ancient independence, perhaps, flitted across his mind.

Cortés, while he encouraged the idea that his own sovereign was the great Being indicated by Montezuma, endeavoured to comfort the monarch by the assurance that his master had no desire to interfere with his authority, otherwise than, out of pure concern for his welfare, to effect his conversion and that of his people to Christianity. Before the emperor dismissed his visitors he consulted his munificent spirit, as usual, by distributing rich stuffs and trinkets of gold among them, so that the poorest soldier, says Bernal Diaz, one of the party, received at least two heavy collars of the precious metal for his share. The iron hearts of the Spaniards were touched with the emotion displayed by Montezuma, as well as by his princely spirit of liberality. As they passed him, the cavaliers, with bonnet in hand, made him the most profound obeisance, and "on the way home," continues the same chronicler, "we could discourse of nothing but the gentle breeding and courtesy of the Indian monarch, and of the respect we entertained for him."

Speculations of a graver complexion must have pressed on the mind of the general, as he saw around him the evidences of a civilization, and consequently power, for which even the exaggerated reports of the natives – discredited from their apparent exaggeration – had not prepared him. In the pomp and burdensome ceremonial of the court, he saw that nice system of subordination and profound reverence for the monarch which characterize the semi-civilized empires of Asia. In the appearance of the capital, its massy, yet elegant architecture, its luxurious social accommodations, its activity in trade, he recognised the proofs of the intellectual progress, mechanical skill, and enlarged resources of an old and opulent community; while the swarms in the streets attested the existence of a population capable of turning those resources to the best account.

In the Aztec he beheld a being unlike either the rude republican Tlascalan, or the effeminate Cholulan; but combining the courage of the one with the cultivation of the other. He was in the heart of a great capital, which seemed like an extensive fortification, with its dikes and its drawbridges, where every house might be easily converted into a castle. Its insular position removed it from the continent, from which, at the mere nod of the sovereign, all communication might be cut off, and the whole warlike population be at once precipitated on him and his handful of followers. What could superior science avail against such odds?

As to the subversion of Montezuma's empire, now that he had seen him in his capital, it must have seemed a more doubtful enterprise than ever. The recognition which the Aztec prince had made of the feudal supremacy, if I may so say, of the Spanish sovereign, was not to be taken too literally. Whatever show of deference he might be disposed to pay the latter, under the influence of his present – perhaps temporary – delusion, it was not to be supposed that he would so easily relinquish his actual power and possessions, or that his people would consent to it. Indeed, his sensitive apprehensions in regard to this very subject, on the coming of the Spaniards, were sufficient proof of the tenacity with which he clung to his authority. It is true that Cortés had a strong lever for future operations in the superstitious reverence felt for himself both by prince and people. It was undoubtedly his policy to maintain this sentiment unimpaired in both, as far as possible. But, before settling any plan of operations, it was necessary to make himself personally acquainted with the topography and local advantages of the capital, the character of its population, and the real nature and amount of its resources. With this view, he asked the emperor's permission to visit the principal public edifices.

The friendly monarch consented without difficulty. He even prepared to go in person to the great temple, to receive his guests there, – it may be, to shield the shrine of his tutelar deity from any attempted profanation. Cortés put himself at the head of his little corps of cavalry, and nearly all the Spanish foot, as usual, and followed the caciques sent by Montezuma to guide him. They proposed first to conduct him to the great market of Tlatelolco in the western part of the city.

The *teocalli* [Great Temple] was a solid pyramidal structure of earth and pebbles, coated on the outside with hewn stones, probably of the light, porous kind employed in the buildings of the city. It was probably square, with its sides facing the cardinal points. It was divided into five bodies or stories, each one receding so as to be of smaller dimensions than that immediately below it. The ascent was by a flight of steps on the outside, which reached to the narrow terrace or platform at the base of the second story, passing quite round the building, when a second stairway conducted to a similar landing at the base of the third. The breadth of the walk was just so much space as was left by the retreating story next above it. From this construction the visitor was obliged to pass round the whole edifice four times, in order to reach

45

the top. This had a most imposing effect in the religious ceremonials, when the pompous procession of priests with their wild minstrelsy came sweeping round the huge sides of the pyramid, as they rose higher and higher, in the presence of gazing multitudes, towards the summit.

The dimensions of the temple cannot be given with any certainty. The Conquerors judged by the eye, rarely troubling themselves with any thing like an accurate measurement. It was, probably, not much less than three hundred feet square at the base; and, as the Spaniards counted a hundred and fourteen steps, was probably, less than one hundred feet in height.

When Cortés arrived before the *teocalli*, he found two priests and several caciques commissioned by Montezuma to save him the fatigue of the ascent by bearing him on their shoulders, in the same manner as had been done to the emperor. But the general declined the compliment, preferring to march up at the head of his men. On reaching the summit, they found it a vast area, paved with broad flat stones. The first object that met their view was a large block of jasper, the peculiar shape of which showed it was the stone on which the bodies of the unhappy victims were stretched for sacrifice. Its convex surface, by raising the breast, enabled the priest to perform his diabolical task more easily, of removing the heart. At the other end of the area were two towers or sanctuaries, consisting of three stories, the lower one of stone and stucco, the two upper of wood elaborately carved. In the lower division stood the images of their gods; the apartments above were filled with utensils for their religious services, and with the ashes of some of their Aztec princes, who had fancied this airy sepulchre. Before each sanctuary stood an altar with that undying fire upon it, the extinction of which boded as much evil to the empire, as that of the Vestal flame would have done in ancient Rome. Here, also, was the huge cylindrical drum made of serpents' skins, and struck only on extraordinary occasions, when it sent forth a melancholy sound that might be heard for miles, – a sound of woe in after times to the Spaniards.

Montezuma, attended by the high priest, came forward to receive Cortés as he mounted the area. "You are weary, Malintzin," said he to him, "with climbing up our great temple." But Cortés, with a politic vaunt, assured him "the Spaniards were never weary!" Then, taking him by the hand, the emperor pointed out the localities of the neighbourhood. The temple on which they stood, rising high above all other edifices in the capital, afforded the most elevated as well as central point of view. The view reached in an unbroken line to the very base of the circular range of mountains, whose frosty peaks glittered as if touched with fire in the morning ray; while long, dark wreaths of vapor, rolling up from the hoary head of Popocatepetl, told that the destroying element was, indeed, at work in the bosom of the beautiful Valley.

Cortés was filled with admiration at this grand and glorious spectacle, and gave utterance to his feelings in animated language to the emperor, the lord of these flourishing domains. His thoughts, however, soon took another direction; and, turning to father Olmedo, who stood by his side, he suggested that the area would afford a most conspicuous position for the Christian Cross, if Montezuma would but allow it to be planted there. But the discreet ecclesiastic, with the good sense which on these occasions seems to have been so lamentably deficient in his commander, reminded him, that such a request, at present, would be exceedingly ill-timed, as the Indian monarch had shown no dispositions as yet favourable to Christianity.

Cortés then requested Montezuma to allow him to enter the sanctuaries, and behold the shrines of his gods. To this the latter, after a short conference with the priests, assented, and conducted the Spaniards into the building. They found themselves in a spacious apartment incrusted on the sides with stucco, on which various figures were sculptured, representing the Mexican calendar, perhaps, or the priestly ritual. At one end of the saloon was a recess with a roof of timber richly carved and gilt. Before the altar in this sanctuary, stood the colossal image of Huitzilopotchli, the tutelary deity and war-god of the Aztecs. His countenance was distorted into hideous lineaments of symbolical import. In his right hand he wielded a bow, and in his left a bunch of golden arrows, which a mystic legend had connected with the victories of his people. The huge folds of a serpent, consisting of pearls and precious stones, were coiled round his waist, and the same rich materials were profusely sprinkled over his person. On his left foot were the delicate feathers of the humming-bird, which, singularly enough, gave its name to the dread deity. The most conspicuous ornament was a chain of gold and silver hearts alternate, suspended around his neck, emblematical of the sacrifice in which he most delighted. A more unequivocal evidence of this was afforded by three human hearts smoking and almost palpitating, as if recently torn from the victims, and now lying on the altar before him!

The adjoining sanctuary was dedicated to a milder deity. This was Tezcatlipoca, next in honor to that invisible Being, the Supreme God, who was represented by no image, and confined by no temple. It was Tezcatlipoca who created the world, and watched over it with a prudential care. He was represented as a young man, and his image, of polished black stone, was richly garnished with gold plates and ornaments; among which a shield, burnished like a mirror, was the most characteristic emblem, as in it he saw reflected all the doings of the world. But the homage to this god was not always of a more refined or merciful character than that paid to his carnivorous brother; for five bleeding hearts were also seen in a golden platter on his altar.

The walls of both these chapels were stained with human gore. "The stench was more intolerable" exclaims Diaz, "than that of the slaughter-houses in Castile!" And the frantic forms of the priests, with their dark robes clotted with blood, as they flitted to and fro, seemed to the Spaniards to be those of the very ministers of Satan!

From this foul abode they gladly escaped into the open air; when Cortés, turning to Montezuma, said with a smile, "I do not comprehend how a great and wise prince, like you, can put faith in such evil spirits as these idols, the representatives of the Devil! If you will but permit us to erect here the true Cross, and place the images of the blessed Virgin and her Son in your sanctuaries, you will soon see how your false gods will shrink before them!"

Montezuma was greatly shocked at this sacrilegious address. "These are the gods," he answered, "who have led the Aztecs on to victory since they were a nation, and who send the seed-time and harvest in their seasons. Had I thought you would have offered them this outrage, I would not have admitted you into their presence."

Cortés, after some expressions of concern at having wounded the feelings of the emperor, took his leave. Montezuma remained, saying that he must expiate, if possible, the crime of exposing the shrines of the divinities to such profanation by the strangers.

On descending to the court, the Spaniards took a leisurely survey of the other edifices in the inclosure. Among the *teocallis* in the inclosure was one consecrated to Quetzalcoatl, circular in its form, and having an entrance in imitation of a dragon's mouth, bristling with sharp fangs, and dropping with blood. As the Spaniards cast a furtive glance into the throat of this horrible monster, they saw collected there implements of sacrifice and other abominations of fearful import. Their bold hearts shuddered at the spectacle, and they designated the place not inaptly as the "Hell."

The sight of the Indian abominations seems to have kindled in the Spaniards a livelier feeling for their own religion; since, on the following day, they asked leave of Montezuma to convert one of the halls in their residence into a chapel, that they might celebrate the services of the Church there. The monarch, in whose bosom the feelings of resentment seem to have soon subsided, easily granted their request, and sent some of his own artisans to aid them in the work.

While it was in progress, some of the Spaniards observed what appeared to be a door recently plastered over. It was a common rumor that Montezuma still kept the treasure of his father, King Ayaxacatl, in this ancient palace. The Spaniards, acquainted with this fact, felt no scruple in gratifying their curiosity by removing the plaster. As was anticipated, it concealed a door. On forcing this, they found the rumor was no exaggeration. They beheld a large hall filled with rich and beautiful stuffs, articles of curious workmanship of various kinds, gold and silver in bars and in the ore, and many jewels of value. It was the private hoard of Montezuma, the contributions, it may be, of tributary cities, and once the property of his father. "I was a young man," says Diaz, who was one of those that obtained a sight of it, "and it seemed to me as if all the riches of the world were in that room!" The Spaniards, notwithstanding their elation at the discovery of this precious deposit, seem to have felt some commendable scruples as to appropriating it to their own use, – at least for the present. And Cortés, after closing up the wall as it was before, gave strict instructions that nothing should be said of the matter, unwilling that the knowledge of its existence by his guests should reach the ears of Montezuma.

Three days sufficed to complete the chapel; and the Christians had the satisfaction to see themselves in possession of a temple where they might worship God in their own way, under the protection of the Cross, and the blessed Virgin. Mass was regularly performed by the fathers Olmedo and Diaz, in the presence of the assembled army, who were most earnest and exemplary in their devotions, partly, says the chronicler above quoted, from the propriety of the thing, and partly for its edifying influence on the benighted heathen.

The Spaniards had been now a week in Mexico. During this time, they had experienced the most friendly treatment from the emperor. But the mind of Cortés was far from easy. He felt that it was quite uncertain how long this amiable temper would last. A hundred circumstances might occur to change it. He might very naturally feel the maintenance of so large a body too burdensome on his treasury. The people of the capital might become dissatisfied at the presence of so numerous an armed force within their walls. Many causes of disgust might arise betwixt the soldiers and the citizens. Indeed, it was scarcely possible that a rude, licentious soldiery, like the Spaniards, could be long kept in subjection without active employment. The danger was even greater with the Tlascalans, a fierce race now brought into daily contact with the nation who held them in loathing and detestation. Rumours were already rife among the allies, whether well-founded or not, of murmurs among the Mexicans, accompanied by menaces of raising the bridges.

Even should the Spaniards be allowed to occupy their present quarters unmolested, it was not advancing the great object of the expedition. Cortés was not a whit nearer gaining the capital, so essential to his meditated subjugation of the country; and any day he might receive tidings that the Crown, or, what he most feared, the governor of Cuba, had sent a force of superior strength to wrest from him a conquest but half achieved. Disturbed by these anxious reflections, he resolved to extricate himself from his embarrassment by one bold stroke. But he first submitted the affair to a council of the officers in whom he most confided, desirous to divide with them the responsibility of the act, and, no doubt, to interest them more heartily in its execution, by making it in some measure the result of their combined judgments.

When the general had briefly stated the embarrassments of their position, the council was divided in opinion. All admitted the necessity of some instant action. One party were for retiring secretly from the city, and getting beyond the causeways before their march could be intercepted. Another advised that it should be done openly, with the knowledge of the emperor, of whose good-will they had had so many proofs. But both these measures seemed alike impolitic. A retreat under these circumstances, and so abruptly made, would have the air of a flight. It would be construed into distrust of themselves; and any thing like timidity on their part would be sure not only to bring on them the Mexicans, but the contempt of their allies, who would, doubtless, join in the general cry.

As to Montezuma, what reliance could they place on the protection of a prince so recently their enemy, and who, in his altered bearing, must have taken counsel of his fears, rather than his inclinations?

Even should they succeed in reaching the coast, their situation would be little better. It would be proclaiming to the world, that, after all their lofty vaunts, they were unequal to the enterprise. Their only hopes of their sovereign's favour, and of pardon for their irregular proceedings, were founded on success. Hitherto, they had only made the discovery of Mexico; to retreat would be to leave conquest and the fruits of it to another. – In short, to stay and to retreat seemed equally disastrous.

In this perplexity, Cortés proposed an expedient, which none but the most daring spirit, in the most desperate extremity, would have conceived. This was, to march to the royal palace, and bring Montezuma to the Spanish quarters, by fair means if they could persuade him, by force if necessary, – at all events, to get possession of his person. With such a pledge, the Spaniards would be secure from the assault of the Mexicans, afraid by acts of violence to compromise the safety of their prince. If he came by his own consent, they would be deprived of all apology for doing so. As long as the emperor remained among the Spaniards, it would be easy, by allowing him a show of sovereignty, to rule in his name, until they had taken measures for securing their safety, and the success of their enterprise. The idea of employing a sovereign as a tool for the government of his own kingdom, if a new one in the age of Cortés, is certainly not so in ours.

A plausible pretext for the seizure of the hospitable monarch – for the most barefaced action seeks to veil itself under some show of decency – was afforded by a circumstance of which Cortés had received intelligence at Cholula. He had left a faithful officer, Juan de Escalante, with a hundred and fifty men in garrison at Vera Cruz, on his departure for the capital. He had not been long absent, when his lieutenant received a message from an Aztec chief named Quauhpopoca, governor of a district to the north of the Spanish settlement, declaring his desire to come in person and tender his allegiance to the Spanish authorities at Vera Cruz. He requested that four of the white men might be sent to protect him against certain unfriendly tribes through which his road lay. This was not an uncommon request, and excited no suspicion in Escalante. The four soldiers were sent; and on their arrival two of them were murdered by the false Aztec. The other two made their way back to the garrison.

The commander marched at once, with fifty of his men, and several thousand Indian allies, to take vengeance on the cacique. A pitched battle followed. The allies fled from the redoubted Mexicans. The few Spaniards stood firm, and with the aid of their firearms and the blessed Virgin, who was distinctly seen hovering over their ranks in the van, they made good the field against the enemy. It cost them dear, however; since seven or eight Christians were slain, and among them the gallant Escalante himself, who died of his injuries soon after his return to the fort. The Indian prisoners captured in the battle spoke of the whole proceeding as having taken place at the instigation of Montezuma.

One of the Spaniards fell into the hands of the natives, but soon after perished of his wounds. His head was cut off and sent to the Aztec emperor. It was uncommonly large and covered with hair; and, as Montezuma gazed on the ferocious features, rendered more horrible by death, he seemed to read in them the dark lineaments of the destined destroyers of his house. He turned from it with a shudder, and commanded that it should be taken from the city, and not offered at the shrine of any of his gods.

Although Cortés had received intelligence of this disaster at Cholula, he had concealed it within his own breast, or communicated it to very few only of his most trusty officers, from apprehension of the ill effect it might have on the spirits of the common soldiers.

The cavaliers whom Cortés now summoned to the council were men of the same mettle with their leader. Their bold, chivalrous spirits seemed to court danger for its own sake. If one or two, less adventurous, were startled by the proposal he made, they were soon overruled by the others, who, no doubt, considered that a desperate disease required as desperate a remedy.

That night, Cortés was heard pacing his apartment to and fro, like a man oppressed by thought, or agitated by strong emotion. He may have been ripening in his mind the daring scheme for the morrow. In the morning the soldiers heard mass as usual, and father Olmedo invoked the blessing of Heaven on their hazardous enterprise. Whatever might be the cause in which he was embarked, the heart of the Spaniard was cheered with the conviction that the Saints were on his side!

Having asked an audience from Montezuma, which was readily granted, the general made the necessary arrangements for his enterprise. The principal part of his force was drawn up in the court-yard, and he stationed a considerable detachment in the avenues leading to the palace, to check any attempt at rescue by the populace. He ordered twenty-five or thirty of the soldiers to drop in at the palace, as if by accident, in groups of three or four at a time, while the conference was going on with Montezuma. He selected five cavaliers, in whose courage and coolness he placed most trust, to bear him company; Pedro de Alvarado, Gonzalo de Sandoval, Francisco de Lujo, Velasquez de Leon, and Alonso de Avila, – brilliant names in the annals of the Conquest. All were clad, as well as the common soldiers, in complete armor, a circumstance of too familiar occurrence to excite suspicion.

The little party were graciously received by the emperor, who soon, with the aid of the interpreters, became interested in a sportive conversation with the Spaniards, while he indulged his natural munificence by giving them presents of gold and jewels. He paid the Spanish general the particular compliment of offering him one of his daughters as his wife; an honor which the latter respectfully declined, on the ground that he was already accommodated with one in

Cuba, and that his religion forbade a plurality.

When Cortés perceived that a sufficient number of his soldiers were assembled, he changed his playful manner, and with a serious tone briefly acquainted Montezuma with the treacherous proceedings in the *tierra caliente*, and the accusation of him as their author. The emperor listened to the charge with surprise; and disavowed the act, which he said could only have been imputed to him by his enemies. Cortés expressed his belief in his declaration, but added, that, to prove it true, it would be necessary to send for Quauhpopoca and his accomplices, that they might be examined and dealt with according to their deserts. To this Montezuma made no objection. Taking from his wrist, to which it was attached, a precious stone, the royal signet, on which was cut the figure of the War-god, he gave it to one of his nobles, with orders to show it to the Aztec governor, and require his instant presence in the capital, together with all those who had been accessory to the murder of the Spaniards. If he resisted, the officer was empowered to call in the aid of the neighbouring towns, to enforce the mandate.

When the messenger had gone, Cortés assured the monarch that this prompt compliance with his request convinced him of his innocence. But it was important that his own sovereign should be equally convinced of it. Nothing would promote this so much as for Montezuma to transfer his residence to the palace occupied by the Spaniards, till on the arrival of Quauhpopoca the affair could be fully investigated. Such an act of condescension would, of itself, show a personal regard for the Spaniards, incompatible with the base conduct alleged against him, and would fully absolve him from all suspicion!

Montezuma listened to this proposal, and the flimsy reasoning with which it was covered, with looks of profound amazement. He became pale as death; but in a moment, his face flushed with resentment, as, with the pride of offended dignity, he exclaimed, "When was it ever heard that a great prince, like myself, voluntarily left his own palace to become a prisoner in the hands of strangers!"

Cortés assured him he would not go as a prisoner. He would experience nothing but respectful treatment from the Spaniards; would be surrounded by his own household, and hold intercourse with his people as usual. In short, it would be but a change of residence, from one of his palaces to another, a circumstance of frequent occurrence with him. – It was in vain. "If I should consent to such a degradation," he answered, "my subjects never would!" When further pressed, he offered to give up one of his sons and of his daughters to remain as hostages with the Spaniards, so that he might be spared this disgrace.

Two hours passed in this fruitless discussion, till a high-mettled cavalier, Velasquez de Leon, impatient of the long delay, and seeing that the attempt, if not the deed, must ruin them, cried out, "Why do we waste words on this barbarian? We have gone too far to recede now. Let us seize him, and if he resists, plunge our swords into his body!" The fierce tone and menacing gestures, with which this was uttered, alarmed the monarch, who inquired of Marina what the angry Spaniard said. The interpreter explained it in as gentle a manner as she could, beseeching him "to accompany the white men to their quarters, where he would be treated with all respect and kindness, while to refuse them would be expose himself to violence, perhaps to death." Marina, doubtless, spoke to her sovereign as she thought, and no one had better opportunity of knowing the truth than herself.

This last appeal shook the resolution of Montezuma. It was in vain that the unhappy prince looked around for sympathy or support. As his eyes wandered over the stern visages and iron forms of the Spaniards, he felt that his hour was indeed come; and, with a voice scarcely audible from emotion, he consented to accompany the strangers, to quit the palace, whither he was never more to return. Had he possessed the spirit of the first Montezuma, he would have called his guards around him, and left his life-blood on the threshold, sooner than have been dragged a dishonoured captive across it. But his courage sank under circumstances. He felt he was the instrument of an irresistible Fate!

No sooner had the Spaniards got his consent, than orders were given for the royal litter. The nobles, who bore and attended it, could scarcely believe their senses, when they learned their master's purpose. But pride now came to Montezuma's aid, and, since he must go, he preferred that it should appear to be with his own free will. As the royal retinue, escorted by the Spaniards, marched through the street with downcast eyes and dejected mien, the people assembled in crowds, and a rumor ran among them, that the emperor was carried off by force to the quarters of the white men. A tumult would have soon arisen but for the intervention of Montezuma himself, who called out to the people to disperse, as he was visiting his friends of his own accord; thus sealing his ignominy by a declaration which deprived his subjects of the only excuse for resistance. On reaching the quarters, he sent out his nobles with similar assurances to the mob, and renewed orders to return to their homes.

He was received with ostentatious respect by the Spaniards, and selected the suite of apartments which best pleased him. They were soon furnished with fine cotton tapestries, feather-work and all the elegances of Indian upholstery. He was attended by such of his household as he chose, his wives and his pages, and was served with his usual pomp and luxury at his meals. He gave audience, as in his own palace, to his subjects, who were admitted to his presence, few, indeed, at a time, under the pretext of greater order and decorum. From the Spaniards themselves he met with a formal deference. No one, not even the general himself, approached him without doffing his casque, and rendering the obeisance due to his rank. Nor did they ever sit in his presence, without being invited by him to do so.

With all this studied ceremony and show of homage, there was once circumstance which too clearly proclaimed to his people that their sovereign was a prisoner. In the front of the palace a patrol of sixty men was established, and the same number in the rear. Twenty of each corps mounted guard at once, maintaining a careful watch, day and night. Another body, under command of Velasquez de Leon, was stationed in the royal antechamber. Cortés punished any departure from duty, or relaxation of vigilance, in these sentinels, with the utmost severity. He felt, as, indeed, every Spaniard must have felt, that the escape of the emperor now would be their ruin. Yet the task of this unintermitting watch sorely added to their fatigues. "Better this dog of a king should die," cried a soldier one day, "than that we should wear out our lives in this manner." The words were uttered in the hearing of Montezuma, who gathered something of their import, and the offender was severely chastised by order of the general.

Such instances of disrespect, however, were very rare. Indeed, the amiable deportment of the monarch, who seemed to take pleasure in the society of his jailers, and who never allowed a favor or attention from the meanest soldier to go unrequited, inspired the Spaniards with as much attachment as they were capable of feeling – for a barbarian.

Things were in this posture, when the arrival of Quauhpopoca from the coast was announced. He was accompanied by his son and fifteen Aztec chiefs. He had travelled all the way, borne, as became his high rank, in a litter. On entering Montezuma's presence, he threw over his dress the coarse robe of *nequen*, and made the usual humiliating acts of obeisance. The poor parade of courtly ceremony was the more striking, when placed on contrast with the actual condition of the parties.

The Aztec governor was coldly received by his master, who referred the affair (had he the power to do otherwise?) to the examination of Cortés. It was, doubtless, conducted in a sufficiently summary manner. To the general's query, whether the cacique was the subject of Montezuma, he replied, "And what other sovereign could I serve?" implying that his sway was universal. He did not deny his share in the transaction, nor did he seek to shelter himself under the royal authority, till sentence of death was passed on him and his followers, when they all laid the blame of their proceedings on Montezuma. They were condemned to be burnt alive in the area before the palace. The funeral piles were made of heaps of arrows, javelins, and other weapons, drawn by the emperor's permission from the arsenals round the great *teocalli*, where they had been stored to supply means of defence in times of civic tumult or insurrection. By this politic precaution, Cortés proposed to remove a ready means of annoyance in case of hostilities with the citizens.

To crown the whole of these extraordinary proceedings, Cortés, while preparations for the execution were going on, entered the emperor's apartment, attended by a soldier bearing fetters in his hands. With a severe aspect, he charged the monarch with being the original contriver of the violence offered to the Spaniards, as was now proved by the declaration of his own instruments. Such a crime, which merited death in a subject, could not be atoned for, even by a sovereign, without some punishment. So saying, he ordered the soldier to fasten the fetters on Montezuma's ankles. He coolly waited till it was done; then, turning his back on the monarch, quitted the room.

Montezuma was speechless under the infliction of this last insult. He was like one struck down by a heavy blow, that deprives him of all his faculties. He offered no resistance. But, though he spoke not a word, low, ill-suppressed moans, from time to time, intimated the anguish of his spirit. His attendants, bathed in tears, offered him their consolations. They tenderly held his feet in their arms, and endeavoured, by inserting their shawls and mantles, to relieve them from the pressure of the iron. But they could not reach the iron which had penetrated his soul. He felt that he was no more a king.

Meanwhile, the execution of the dreadful doom was going forward in the court-yard. The whole Spanish force was under arms, to check any interruption that might be offered by the Mexicans. But none was attempted. The populace gazed in silent wonder, regarding it as the sentence of the emperor. The manner of the execution, too, excited less surprise, from their familiarity with similar spectacles, aggravated, indeed, by additional horrors, in their own diabolical sacrifices. The Aztec lord and his companions, bound hand and foot to the blazing piles, submitted without a cry or a complaint to their terrible fate. Passive fortitude is the virtue of the Indian warrior; and it was the glory of the Aztec, as of the other races on the North American continent, to show how the spirit of the brave man may triumph over torture and the agonies of death.

When the dismal tragedy was ended, Cortés re-entered Montezuma's apartment. Kneeling down, he unclasped the shackles with his own hand, expressing at the same time his regret that so disagreeable a duty as that of subjecting him to such a punishment had been imposed on him. This last indignity had entirely crushed the spirit of Montezuma; and the monarch, whose frown, but a week since, would have made the nations of Anahuac tremble to their remotest borders, was now craven enough to thank his deliverer for his freedom, as for a great and unmerited boon!

Not long after, the Spanish general, conceiving that his royal captive was sufficiently humbled, expressed his willingness that he should return, if he inclined, to his own palace. Montezuma declined it; alleging, it is said, that his nobles had more than once importuned him to resent his injuries by taking arms against the Spaniards; and that, were he in the midst of them, it would be difficult to avoid it, or to save his capital from bloodshed and anarchy. The reason did honor to his heart, if it was the one which influenced him. It is probable that he did not care to trust his safety to those haughty and ferocious chieftains, who had witnessed the degradation of their master, and must despise his pusillanimity, as thing unprecedented in an Aztec monarch.

1520.

Notwithstanding the actual control exercised by the Spaniards through their royal captive, Cortés felt some uneasiness, when he reflected that it was in the power of the Indians, at any time, to cut off his communications with the surrounding country, and hold him a prisoner in the capital. He proposed, therefore, to build two vessels of sufficient size to transport his forces across the lake, and thus to render himself independent of the causeways. Montezuma was pleased with the idea of seeing these wonderful "water-houses", of which he had heard so much, and readily gave permission to have the timber in the royal forests felled for the purpose. The work was placed under the direction of Martin Lopez, an experienced ship-builder. Orders were also given to Sandoval to send up from the coast a supply of cordage, sails, iron, and other necessary materials, which had been judiciously saved on the destruction of the fleet.

The Aztec emperor, meanwhile, was passing his days in the Spanish quarters in no very different manner from what he had been accustomed to in his own palace. His keepers were too well aware of the value of their prize, not to do every thing which could make his captivity comfortable, and disguise it from himself. But the chain will gall, though wreathed with roses. After Montezuma's breakfast, which was a light meal of fruits or vegetables, Cortés or some of his officers usually waited on him, to learn if he had any commands for them. He then devoted some time to business. He gave audience to those of his subjects who had petitions to prefer, or suits to settle. The statement of the party was drawn up on the hieroglyphic scrolls, which were submitted to a number of counsellors or judges, who assisted him with their advice on these occasions. Envoys from foreign states or his own remote provinces and cities were also admitted, and the Spaniards were careful that the same precise and punctilious etiquette should be maintained towards the royal puppet, as when in the plenitude of his authority.

After business was despatched, Montezuma often amused himself with seeing the Castilian troops go through their military exercises. He, too, had been a soldier, and in his prouder days had led armies in the field. It was very natural he should take an interest in the novel display of European tactics and discipline. At other times he would challenge Cortés or his officers to play at some of the national games. A favorite one was called *totoloque*, played with golden balls aimed at a target or mark of the same metal. Montezuma usually staked something of value, – precious stones or ingots of gold. He lost with good humor; indeed it was of little consequence whether he won or lost, since he generally gave away his winnings to his attendants. He had, in truth, a most munificent spirit. His enemies accused him of avarice. But, if he were avaricious, it could have been only that he might have the more to give away.

Each of the Spaniards had several Mexicans, male and female, who attended to his cooking and various other personal offices. Cortés, considering that the maintenance of this host of menials was a heavy tax on the royal exchequer, ordered them to be dismissed, excepting one to be retained for each soldier. Montezuma, on learning this, pleasantly remonstrated with the general on his careful economy, as unbecoming a royal establishment, and, countermanding the order, caused additional accommodations to be provided for the attendants, and their pay to be doubled.

On another occasion, a solider purloined some trinkets of gold from the treasure kept in the chamber, which, since Montezuma's arrival in the Spanish quarters, had been reopened. Cortés would have punished the man for the theft, but the emperor interfering said to him, "Your countrymen are welcome to the gold and other articles, if you will but spare those belonging to the gods." Some of the soldiers, making the most of his permission, carried off several hundred loads of fine cotton to their quarters. When this was represented to Montezuma, he only replied, "What I have once given, I never take back again."

While thus indifferent to his treasures, he was keenly sensitive to personal slight or insult. When a common soldier once spoke to him angrily, the tears came into the monarch's eyes, as it made him feel the true character of his impotent condition. Cortés, on becoming acquainted with it, was so much incensed, that he ordered the soldier to be hanged; but, on Montezuma's intercession, commuted this severe sentence for a flogging. The general was not willing that any one but himself should treat his royal captive with indignity. Montezuma was desired to procure a further mitigation of the punishment. But he refused, saying, "that, if a similar insult had been offered by any one of his subjects to Malintzin, he would have resented it in like manner."

Such instances of disrespect were very rare. Montezuma's amiable and inoffensive manners, together with his liberality, the most popular of virtues with the vulgar, made him generally beloved of the Spaniards. The arrogance, for which he had been so distinguished in his prosperous days, deserted him in his fallen fortunes. His character in captivity seems to have undergone something of that change which takes place in the wild animals of the forest, when caged within the walls of the menagerie.

The Indian monarch knew the name of every man in the army, and was careful to discriminate his proper rank. For some he showed a strong partiality. He obtained from the general a favorite page, named Orteguilla, who, being in constant attendance on his person, soon learned enough of the Mexican language to be of use to his countrymen. Montezuma took great pleasure, also, in the society of Velasquez de Leon, the captain of his guard, and Pedro de Alvarado, *Tonatiuh*, or "the Sun," as he was called by the Aztecs, from his yellow hair and sunny countenance. The sunshine, as events afterwards showed, could sometimes be the prelude to a terrible tempest.

Notwithstanding the care taken to cheat him of the tedium of captivity, the royal prisoner cast a wistful glance, now and then, beyond the walls of his residence to the ancient haunts of business or pleasure. He intimated a desire to offer up his devotions at the great temple, where he was once so constant in his worship. The suggestion startled Cortés. It was too reasonable, however, for him to object to it, without wholly discarding the appearances which he was desirous to maintain. But he secured Montezuma's return by sending an escort with him of a hundred and fifty soldiers under the same resolute cavaliers who had aided in his seizure. He told him, also, that, in case of any attempt to escape, his life would instantly pay the forfeit. Thus guarded, the Indian prince visited the *teocalli*, where he was received with the usual state, and, after performing his devotions, he returned again to his quarters.

It may well be believed that the Spaniards did not neglect the opportunity afforded by his residence with them, of instilling into him some notions of the Christian doctrine. Fathers Diaz and Olmedo exhausted all their battery of logic and persuasion, to shake his faith in his idols, but in vain. He, indeed, paid a most edifying attention, which gave promise of better things. But the conferences always closed with the declaration that, "the God of the Christians was good, but the gods of his own country were the true gods for him." It is said, however, they extorted a promise from him, that he would take part in no more human sacrifices. Yet such sacrifices were of daily occurrence in the great temples of the capital; and the people were too blindly attached to their own abominations, for the Spaniards to deem it safe for the present at least, openly to interfere.

Montezuma showed, also, an inclination to engage in the pleasures of the chase, of which he once was immoderately fond. He had large forests reserved for the purpose on the other side of the lake. As the Spanish brigantines were now completed, Cortés proposed to transport him and his suite across the water in them. They were of a good size, strongly built. The largest was mounted with four falconets, or small guns. It was protected by a gaily-colored awning stretched over the deck, and the royal ensign of Castile floated proudly from the mast. On board of this vessel, Montezuma, delighted with the opportunity of witnessing the nautical skill of the white men, embarked with a train of Aztec nobles and a numerous guard of Spaniards. A fresh breeze played on the waters, and the vessel soon left behind it the swarms of light pirogues which darkened their surface. She seemed like a thing of life in the eyes of the astonished natives, who saw her, as if disdaining human agency, sweeping by with snowy pinions as if on the wings of the wind, while the thunders from her sides, now for the first time breaking on the silence of this "inland sea", showed that the beautiful phantom was clothed in terror.

The royal chase was well stocked with game; some of which the emperor shot with arrows, and others were driven by the numerous attendants into nets. In these woodland exercises, while he ranged over his wild domain, Montezuma seemed to enjoy again the sweets of liberty. It was but the shadow of liberty, however; as in his quarters, at home, he enjoyed but the shadow of royalty. At home or abroad, the eye of the Spaniard was always upon him.

But, while he resigned himself without a struggle to his inglorious fate, there were others who looked on it with very different emotions. Among them was his nephew Cacama, lord of Tezcuco, a young man not more than twenty-five years of age, but who enjoyed great consideration from his high personal qualities, especially his intrepidity of character. He was the same prince who had been sent by Montezuma to welcome the Spaniards on their entrance to the Valley; and, when the question of their reception was first debated in the council, he had advised to admit them honorably as ambassadors of a foreign prince, and, if they should prove different from what they pretended, it would be time enough then to take up arms against them. That time, he thought, had now come.

The young Tezucan chief beheld, with indignation, and no slight contempt, the abject condition of his uncle. He endeavoured to rouse him to manly exertion, but in vain. He then set about forming a league with several of the neighbouring caciques to rescue his kinsman, and to break the detested yoke of the strangers. He called on the lord of Iztapalapan, Montezuma's brother, the lord of Tlacopan, and some others of most authority, all of whom entered heartily into his views. He then urged the Aztec nobles to join them, but they expressed an unwillingness to take any step not first sanctioned by the emperor. They entertained, undoubtedly, a profound reverence for their master; but it seems probably that jealousy of the personal views of Cacama had its influence on their determination. Whatever were their motives, it is certain, that, by this refusal, they relinquished the best opportunity ever presented for retrieving their sovereign's independence, and their own.

These intrigues could not be conducted to secretly as not to reach the ears of Cortés, who, with his characteristic promptness, would have marched at once on Tezcuco, and trodden out the spark of "rebellion", before it had time to burst into a flame. But from this he was dissuaded by Montezuma, who represented that Cacama was a man of resolution, backed by a powerful force, and not to be put down without a desperate struggle. He consented, therefore, to negotiate, and sent a message of amicable expostulation to the cacique. He received a haughty answer in return. Cortés rejoined in a more menacing tone, asserting the supremacy of his own sovereign, the emperor of Castile. To this Cacama replied, "He acknowledged no such authority; he knew nothing of the Spanish sovereign nor his people, nor did he wish to know anything of them." Montezuma was not more successful in his application to Cacama to come to Mexico, and allow him to mediate his differences with the Spaniards, with whom he assured the prince he was residing as a friend. But the young lord of Tezcuco was not to be so duped. He understood the position of his uncle, and replied, "that, when he did visit his capital, it would be to rescue it, as well as the emperor himself, and their common gods, from bondage. He should come, not with his hand in his bosom, but on his sword, – to drive out the detested strangers who had brought such dishonor on their country".

Cortés, incensed at this tone of defiance, would again have put himself in motion to punish it, but Montezuma interposed with his more politic arts. He had several of the Tezcucan nobles, he said, in his pay; and it would be easy, through their means, to secure Cacama's person, and thus break up the confederacy, at once, without bloodshed. The maintaining of a corps of stipendiaries in the courts of neighbouring princes was a refinement which showed that the Western barbarian understood the science of political intrigue, as well as some of his royal brethren on the other side of the water.

By the contrivance of these faithless nobles, Cacama was induced to hold a conference, relative to the proposed invasion, in a villa which overhung the Tezcucan lake, not far from his capital. Like most of the principal edifices, it was raised so as to admit the entrance of boats beneath it. In the midst of the conference, Cacama was seized by the conspirators, hurried on board a bark in readiness for the purpose, and transported to Mexico. When brought into Montezuma's presence, the high-spirited chief abated nothing of his proud and lofty bearing. He taxed his uncle with his perfidy, and a pusillanimity so unworthy of his former character, and of the royal house from which he was descended. By the emperor he was referred to Cortés, who, holding royalty but cheap in an Indian prince, put him in fetters.

There was at this time in Mexico a brother of Cacama, a stripling much younger than himself. At the instigation of Cortés, Montezuma, pretending that his nephew had forfeited the sovereignty by his late *rebellion*, declared him to be deposed, and appointed Cuicuitzca in his place. The Aztec sovereigns had always been allowed a paramount authority in questions relating to the succession. But this was a most unwarrantable exercise of it. The Tezcucans acquiesced, however, with a ready ductility, which showed their allegiance hung but lightly on them, or, what is more probable, that they were greatly in awe of the Spaniards; and the new prince was welcomed with acclamations to his capital.

Cortés still wanted to get into his hands the other chiefs who had entered into the confederacy with Cacama. This was no difficult matter. Montezuma's authority was absolute, everywhere but in his own palace. By his command, the caciques were seized, each in his own city, and brought in chains to Mexico, where Cortés placed them in strict confinement with their leader.

He had now triumphed over all his enemies. He had set his feet on the necks of princes; and the great chief of the Aztec empire was but a convenient tool in his hands, for accomplishing his purposes. His first use of this power was, to ascertain the actual resources of the monarchy. He sent several parties of Spaniards, guided by the natives, to explore the regions where gold was obtained. It was gleaned mostly from the beds of rivers, several hundred miles from the capital.

His next objective was, to learn if there existed any good natural harbour for shipping on the Atlantic coast, as the road of Vera Cruz left no protection against the tempests that at certain seasons swept over these seas. Montezuma showed him a chart on which the shores of the Mexican Gulf were laid down with tolerable accuracy. Cortés, after carefully inspecting it, sent a commission, consisting of ten Spaniards, several of them pilots, and some Aztecs, who descended to Vera Cruz, and made a careful survey of the coast for nearly sixty leagues south of that settlement, as far as the great river Coatzacualco, which seemed to offer the best, indeed, the only, accommodations for a safe and suitable harbour. A spot was selected as the site of a fortified post, and the general sent a detachment of a hundred and fifty men under Velasquez de Leon to plant a colony there.

He also obtained a grant of an extensive tract of land, in the fruitful province of Oaxaca, where he proposed to lay put a plantation for the Crown. He stocked it with the different kinds of domesticated animals peculiar to the country, and with such indigenous grains and plants as would afford the best articles for export. He soon had the estate under such cultivation, that he assured his master, the emperor, Charles the Fifth, it was worthy twenty thousand ounces of gold.

Cortés now felt his authority sufficiently assured to demand from Montezuma a formal recognition of the supremacy of the Spanish emperor. The Indian monarch had intimated his willingness to acquiesce in this, on their very first interview. He did not object, therefore, to call together his principal caciques for the purpose. When they were assembled, he made them an address, briefly stating the object of the meeting. They were all acquainted, he said, with the ancient tradition, that the great Being, who had once ruled over the land, had declared, on his departure, that he should return at some future time and resume his sway. That time had now arrived. The white men had come from the quarter where the sun rises, beyond the ocean, to which the good deity had withdrawn. They were sent by their master to reclaim the obedience of his ancient subjects. For himself he was ready to acknowledge his authority. "You have been faithful vassals of mine," continued Montezuma, "during the many years that I have sat on the throne of my fathers. I now expect that you will show me this last act of obedience by acknowledging the great king beyond the waters to be your lord, also, and that you will pay him tribute in the same manner as you have hitherto done to me." As he concluded, his voice was nearly stifled by his emotion, and the tears fell fast down his cheeks.

His nobles, many of whom, coming from a distance, had not kept pace with the changes which had been going on in the capital, were filled with astonishment, as they listened to his words and beheld the voluntary abasement of their master, whom they had hitherto reverenced as the omnipotent lord of Anahuac. They were the more affected, therefore, by the sight of his distress. His will, they told him, had always been their law. It should be so now; and, if he thought the sovereign of the strangers was the ancient lord of their country, they were willing to acknowledge him as such still. The oaths of allegiance were then administered with all due solemnity, attested by the Spaniards present, and a full record of the proceedings was drawn up by the royal notary, to be sent to Spain. There was something deeply touching in the ceremony by which an independent and absolute monarch, in obedience less to the dictates of fear than of conscience, thus relinquished his hereditary rights in favor of an unknown and mysterious power. It even moved those hard men who were thus unscrupulously availing themselves of the confiding ignorance of the natives; and, though "it was in the regular way of their own business," says an old chronicler, "there was not a Spaniard who could look on the spectacle with a dry eye"!

The rumor of these strange proceedings was soon circulated through the capital and the country. Men read in them the finger of Providence. The ancient tradition of Quetzalcoatl was familiar to all; and where it had slept scarcely noticed in the memory, it was now revived with many exaggerated circumstances. It was said to be part of the tradition, that the royal line of the Aztecs was to end with Montezuma; and his name, the literal signification of which is "sad" or "angry lord," was construed into an omen of his evil destiny.

Having thus secured this great feudatory to the crown of Castile, Cortés suggested that it would be well for the Aztec chiefs to send his sovereign such a gratuity as would conciliate his good-will by convincing him of the loyalty of his new vassals. Montezuma consented that his collectors should visit the principal cities and provinces, attended by a number of Spaniards, to receive the customary tributes, in the name of the Castilian sovereign. In a few weeks most of them returned, bringing back large quantities of gold and silver plate, rich stuffs, and the various commodities in which the taxes were usually paid.

The Spaniards gazed with greedy eyes on the display of riches, now their own, which far exceeded all hitherto seen in the New World, and fell nothing short of the *El Dorado* which their glowing imaginations had depicted. It may be, that they felt somewhat rebuked by the contrast which their own avarice presented to the princely munificence of the barbarian chief. At least, they seemed to testify their sense of his superiority by the respectful homage which they rendered him, as they poured forth the fulness of their gratitude. They were not so scrupulous, however, as to manifest any delicacy in appropriating to themselves the donative, a small part of which was to find its way into the royal coffers. They clamored loudly for an immediate division of the spoil, which the general would have postponed till the tributes from the remoter provinces had been gathered in. The goldsmiths of Azcapozalco were sent for to take in pieces the larger and coarser ornaments, leaving untouched those of more delicate workmanship. Three days were consumed in this labor, when the heaps of gold were cast into ingots, and stamped with the royal arms.

The division of the spoil was a work of some difficulty. A perfectly equal division of it among the Conquerors would have given them more than three thousand pounds sterling, a-piece; a magnificent booty! But one-fifth was to be deducted for the Crown. An equal portion was reserved for the general, pursuant to the tenor of his commission. A large sum was then allowed to indemnify him and the governor of Cuba, for the charges of the expedition and the loss of the fleet. The garrison of Vera Cruz was also to be provided for. Ample compensation was made to the principal cavaliers. The cavalry, arquebusiers, and crossbowmen, each received double pay. So that, when the turn of the common soldiers came, there remained not more than a hundred *pesos de oro* for each; a sum so insignificant, in comparison with their expectations, that several refused to accept it.

Loud murmurs now rose among the men. "Was it for this," they said, "that we left our homes and families, periled our lives, submitted to fatigue and famine, and all for so contemptible a pittance! Better to have stayed in Cuba, and contented ourselves with the gains of a safe and easy traffic. When we gave up our share of the gold at Vera Cruz, it was on the assurance that should be amply requited in Mexico. We have, indeed, found the riches we expected; but no sooner seen, than they are snatched from us by the very men who pledged us their faith!" The malecontents even went so far as to accuse their leaders of appropriating to themselves several of the richest ornaments, before the partition had been made; an accusation that receives some countenance from a dispute which arose between Mexia, the treasurer for the Crown, and Valasquez de Leon, a relation of the governor, and a favorite of Cortés. The treasurer accused this cavalier of purloining certain pieces of plate before they were submitted to the royal stamp. From words the parties came to blows. They were good swordsmen; several wounds were given on both sides, and the affair might have ended fatally, but for the interference of Cortés who placed both under arrest.

He then used all his authority and insinuating eloquence to calm the passions of his men. It was a delicate crisis. He was sorry, he said, to see them so unmindful of the duty of loyal soldiers, and cavaliers of the Cross, as to brawl like common banditti over their booty. The division, he assured them, had been made on perfectly fair and equitable principles. As to his own share, it was no more than was warranted by

77

his commission. Yet, if they thought it too much, he was willing to forego his just claims, and divide with the poorest soldier. Gold, however welcome, was not the chief object of his ambition. If it were theirs, they should still reflect, that the present treasure was little in comparison with awaited them hereafter; for had they not the whole country and its mines at their disposal? It was only necessary that they should not give an opening to the enemy, by their discord, to circumvent and to crush them. – With these honeyed words, of which he had good store for all fitting occasions, says an old soldier, for whose benefit, in part, they were intended, he succeeded in calming the storm for the present; while in private he took more effectual means, by presents judiciously administered, to mitigate the discontents of the importunate and refractory.

Cortés seemed now to have accomplished the great objects of the expedition. The Indian monarch had declared himself the feudatory of the Spanish. His authority, his revenues, were at the disposal of the general. The conquest of Mexico seemed to be achieved, and that without a blow. But it was far from being achieved. One important step yet remained to be taken, towards which the Spaniards had hitherto made little progress, – the conversion of the natives. With all the exertions of father Olmedo, backed by the polemic talents of the general, neither Montezuma nor his subjects showed any disposition to abjure the faith of their fathers. The bloody exercises of their religion, on the contrary, were celebrated with all the usual circumstance and pomp of sacrifice before the eyes of the Spaniards.

Unable further to endure these abominations, Cortés, attended by several of his cavaliers, waited on Montezuma.

He told the emperor that the Christians could no longer consent to have the services of their religion shut up within the narrow walls of the garrison. They wished to spread its light far abroad, and to open to the people a full participation in the blessings of Christianity. For this purpose, they requested that the great *teocalli* should be delivered up, as a fit place where their worship might be conducted in the presence of the whole city.

Montezuma listened to the proposal with visible consternation. Amidst all his troubles he had leaned for support on his own faith, and, indeed, it was in obedience to it, that he had shown such deference to the Spaniards as the mysterious messengers predicted by the oracles. "Why," said he, "Malintzin, why will you urge matters to such an extremity, that must surely bring down the vengeance of our gods, and stir up an insurrection among my people, who will never endure this profanation of their temples?"

Cortés, seeing how greatly he was moved, made a sign to his officers to withdraw. When left alone with the interpreters, he told the emperor that he would use his influence to moderate the zeal of his followers, and persuade them to be contented with one of the sanctuaries of the *teocalli*. If that were not granted, they should be obliged to take it by force, and to roll down the images of his false deities in the face of the city. "We fear not for our lives," he added, "for, though our numbers are few, the arm of the true God is over us." Montezuma, much agitated, told him he would confer with the priests.

The result of the conference was favorable to the Spaniards, who were allowed to occupy one of the sanctuaries as a place of worship. The tidings spread great joy throughout the camp.

They might now go forth in open day and publish their religion to the assembled capital. No time was lost in availing themselves of the permission. The sanctuary was cleansed of its disgusting impurities. An altar was raised, surmounted by a crucifix and the image of the Virgin. Instead of the gold and jewels which blazed on the neighbouring Pagan shrine, its walls were decorated with fresh garlands of flowers; and an old soldier was stationed to watch over the chapel, and guard it from intrusion.

When these arrangements were completed, the whole army moved in solemn procession up the winding ascent of the pyramid. Entering the sanctuary, and clustering round its portals, they listened reverentially to the service of the mass, as it was performed by the fathers Olmedo and Diaz. And, as the beautiful *Te Deum* rose towards heaven, Cortés and his soldiers, kneeling on the ground, with tears streaming from their eyes, poured forth their gratitude to the Almighty for this glorious triumph of the Cross.

It was a striking spectacle, – that of these rude warriors lifting up their orisons on the summit of this mountain temple, in the very capital of Heathendom, on the spot especially dedicated to its unhallowed mysteries. Side by side, the Spaniard and the Aztec knelt down in prayer; and the Christian hymn mingled its sweet tones of love and mercy with the wild chant raised by the Indian priest in honor of the war-god of Anahuac! It was an unnatural union, and could not long abide.

The people had borne with patience all the injuries and affronts hitherto put on them by the Spaniards. They had seen their sovereign dragged as a captive from his own palace; his ministers butchered before his eyes; his treasurers seized and appropriated; himself in a manner deposed from his royal supremacy. All this they had seen without a struggle to prevent it. But the profanation of their temples touched a deeper feeling, of which the priesthood were not slow to take advantage.

The first intimation of this change of feeling was gathered from Montezuma himself. Instead of his usual cheerfulness, he appeared grave and abstracted, and instead of seeking, as he was wont, the society of the Spaniards, seemed rather to shun it. It was noticed, too, that conferences were more frequent between him and the nobles, and especially the priests. His little page, Orteguilla, who had now picked up a tolerable acquaintance with the Aztec, contrary to Montezuma's usual practice, was not allowed to attend him at these meetings. These circumstances could not fail to awaken most uncomfortable apprehensions in the Spaniards.

Not many days elapsed, however, before Cortés received an invitation, or rather a summons, from the emperor, to attend him in his apartment. The general went with some feelings of anxiety and distrust, taking with him Olid, captain of the guard, and two or three other trusty cavaliers. Montezuma received them with cold civility, and, turning to the general, told him that all his predictions had come to pass. The gods of his country had been offended by the violation of their temples. They had threatened the priests that they would forsake the city, if the sacrilegious strangers were not driven from it, or rather sacrificed on the altars, in expiation of their crimes. The monarch assure the Christians, it was from regard to their safety that he communicated this; and, "if you have any regard for it yourselves," he concluded, "you will leave the country without delay. I have only to raise my finger, and every Aztec in the land will rise in arms against you." There was no reason to doubt his sincerity. For Montezuma, whatever evils had been brought on him by the white men, held them in reverence as a race more highly gifted than his own, while for several, as we have seen, he had conceived an attachment, flowing, no doubt, from their personal attentions and deference to himself.

Cortés was too much master of his feelings, to show how far he was startled by this intelligence. He replied with admirable coolness that he should regret much to leave the capital so precipitately, when he had no vessels to take him from the country. If it were not for this, there could be no obstacle to his leaving it at once. He should also regret another step to which he should be driven, if he quitted it under these circumstances, – that of taking the emperor along with him.

Montezuma was evidently troubled by this last suggestion. He inquired how long it would take to build the vessels, and finally consented to send a sufficient number of workmen to the coast, to act under the orders of the Spaniards; meanwhile, he would use his authority to restrain the impatience of the people, under the assurance that the white men would leave the land, when the means for it were provided. He kept his word. A large body of Aztec artisans left the capital with the most experienced Castilian ship-builders, and, descending to Vera Cruz, began at once to fell the timber and build a sufficient number of ships to transport the Spaniards back to their own country. The work went forward with apparent alacrity. But those who had the direction of it, it is said, received private instructions from the general, to interpose as many delays as possible, in hopes of receiving in the mean time such reinforcements from Europe, as would enable him to maintain his ground.

The whole aspect of things was now changed in the Castilian quarters. Instead of the security and repose in which the troops had of late indulged, they felt a gloomy apprehension of danger, not the less oppressive to the spirits, that it was scarcely visible to the eye; – like the faint speck just descried above the horizon by the voyager in the tropics, to the common gaze seeming only a summer cloud, but which to the experienced mariner bodes the coming of the hurricane. Every precaution that prudence could devise was taken to meet it. The soldier, as he threw himself on his mats for repose, kept on his armor. He ate, drank, slept, with his weapons by his side. His horse stood ready caparisoned, day and night, with the bridle hanging at the saddle-bow. The guns were carefully planted so as to command the great avenues. The sentinels were doubled, and every man, of whatever rank, took his turn in mounting guard. The garrison was in a state of siege. Such was the uncomfortable position of the army, when in the beginning of May, 1520, six months after their arrival in the capital, tidings came from the coast, which gave greater alarm to Cortés, than even the menaced insurrection of the Aztecs.

Eighteen vessels from Cuba had arrived under the command of Pánfilo de Narváez, sent by Governor Velázquez to arrest Cortés, and take charge of the expedition.

Narvaez now openly proclaimed his intention to march against Cortés, and punish him for his rebellion. He made this vaunt so loudly, that the natives, who had flocked in numbers to the camp, which was soon formed on shore, clearly comprehended that the new comers were not friends, but enemies, of the preceding. Narvaez determined, also, – though in opposition to the counsel of the Spaniard, who quoted the example of Cortés, – to establish a settlement on this unpromising spot; and he made the necessary arrangements to organize a municipality. He was informed by the soldier of the existence of the neighbouring colony at Villa Rica, commanded by Sandoval, and consisting of a few invalids, who, he was assured, would surrender on the first summons. Instead of marching against the place, however, he determined to send a peaceful embassy to display his powers, and demand the submission of the garrison.

Cortés addressed a letter to his rival in the most conciliatory terms. He besought him not to proclaim their animosity to the world, and, by kindling a spirit of insubordination in the natives, unsettle all that had been so far secured. A violent collision must be prejudicial even to the victor, and might be fatal for both. It was only in union that they could look for success. He was ready to greet Narvaez as a brother in arms, to share with him the fruits of conquest, and, if he could produce a royal commission, to submit to his authority. Cortés well knew he had no such commission to show.

The general determined to send a special envoy of his

own. The person selected for this delicate office was father Olmedo, who, through the campaign, had shown a practical good sense, and a talent for affairs, not always to be found in persons of his spiritual calling. He was intrusted with another epistle to Narvaez, of similar import with the preceding. Cortés wrote, also, to the licentiate Ayllon, with whose departure he was not acquainted, and to Andrés de Duero, former secretary of Velasquez, and his own friend, who had come over in the present fleet. Olmedo was instructed to converse with these persons in private, as well as with the principal officers and soldiers, and, as far as possible, to infuse into them a spirit of accommodation. To give greater weight to his arguments, he was furnished with a liberal supply of gold.

During this time, Narvaez had abandoned his original design of planting a colony on the sea-coast, and had crossed the country to Cempoalla, where he had taken up his quarters. He was here when [his envoy] Guevara returned and presented the letter of Cortés.

Narvaez glanced over it with a look of contempt, which was changed into one of stern displeasure, as his envoy enlarged on the resources and formidable character of his rival, counselling him, by all means, to accept his proffers of amity. A different effect was produced on the troops, who listened with greedy ears to the accounts given of Cortés, his frank and liberal manners, which they involuntarily contrasted with those of their own commander, the wealth in his camp, where the humblest private could stake his ingot and chain of gold at play, where all revelled in plenty, and the life of the soldier seemed to be one long holyday. Guevara had been admitted only to the sunny side of the picture.

The impression made by these accounts was confirmed by the presence of Olmedo. The ecclesiastic delivered his missives, in like manner, to Narvaez, who ran through their contents with feelings of anger which found vent in the most opprobrious invectives against his rival; while one of his captains, named Salvatierra, openly avowed his intention to cut of the rebel's ears, and broil them for his breakfast! Such impotent sallies did not alarm the stout-hearted friar, who soon entered into communication with many of the officers and soldiers, whom he found better inclined to an accommodation. His insinuating eloquence, backed by his liberal largesses, gradually opened a way into their hearts, and a party was formed under the very eye of their chief, better affected to his rival's interests than to his own. The intrigue could not be conducted to secretly as wholly to elude the suspicions of Narvaez, who would have arrested Olmedo and placed him under confinement, but for the interposition of Duero. He put a stop to his further machinations by sending him back again to his master. But the poison was left to do its work.

Narvaez made the same vaunt, as at his landing, of his design to march against Cortés and apprehend him as a traitor. The Cempoallans learned with astonishment that their new guests, though the countrymen, were enemies of their former. Narvaez also proclaimed his intention to release Montezuma from captivity, and restore him to his throne. It is said he received a rich present from the Aztec emperor, who entered into a correspondence with him. That Montezuma should have treated him with his usual munificence, supposing him to be the friend of Cortés, is very probable. But that he should have entered into a secret communication, hostile to the general's interests, is too repugnant to the whole tenor of his conduct, to be lightly admitted.

These proceedings did not escape the watchful eye of Sandoval. He gathered the particulars partly from deserters, who fled to Villa Rica, and partly from his own agents, who in the disguise of natives mingled in the enemy's camp. He sent a full account of them to Cortés, acquainted him with the growing defection of the Indians, and urged him to take speedy measures for the defence of Villa Rica, if he would not see it fall into the enemy's hands. The general felt that it was time to act.

Yet the selection of the course to be pursued was embarrassing in the extreme. If he remained in Mexico and awaited there the attack of his rival, it would give the latter time to gather round him the whole forces of the empire, including those of the capital itself, all willing, no doubt, to serve under the banners of a chief who proposed the liberation of their master. The odds were too great to be hazarded.

If he marched against Narvaez, he must either abandon the city and the emperor, the fruit of all his toils and triumphs, or, by leaving a garrison to hold them in awe, must cripple his strength, already far too weak to cope with that of his adversary. Yet on this latter course he decided. He trusted less, perhaps, to an open encounter of arms, than to the influence of his personal address and previous intrigues, to bring about an amicable arrangement. But he prepared himself for either result.

Cortés had sent to the distant province of Chinantla, situated far to the south-east of Cholula, for a reinforcement of two thousand natives. They were a bold race, hostile to the Mexicans, and had offered their services to him since his residence in the metropolis. They used a long spear in battle, longer, indeed than that borne by the Spanish or German infantry. Cortés ordered three hundred of their double-headed lances to be made for him, and to be tipped with copper instead of *itztli*. With this formidable weapon he proposed to foil the cavalry of his enemy.

The command of the garrison, in his absence, he instructed to Pedro de Alvarado, – the *Tonatiuh* of the Mexicans, – a man possessed of many commanding qualities, of an intrepid, though somewhat arrogant spirit, and his warm personal friend. He inculcated on him moderation and forbearance. He was to keep a close watch on Montezuma, for on the possession of the royal person rested all their authority in the land. He was to show him the deference alike due to his high station, and demanded by policy. He was to pay uniform respect to the usages and the prejudices of the people; remembering that though his small force would be large enough to overawe them in times of quiet, yet, should they be once roused, it would be swept away like chaff before the whirlwind.

From Montezuma he exacted a promise to maintain the same friendly relations with his lieutenant which he had preserved towards himself. This, said Cortés, would be most grateful to his own master, the Spanish sovereign. Should the Aztec prince do otherwise, and lend himself to any hostile movement, he must be convinced that he would fall the first victim of it.

The emperor assured him of his continued good-will. He was much perplexed, however, by the recent events.

Were the Spaniards at his court, or those just landed, the true representatives of their sovereign? Cortés, who had hitherto maintained a reserve on the subject, now told him that the latter were indeed his countrymen, but traitors to his master. As such, it was his painful duty to march against them, and, when he had chastised their rebellion, he should return, before his departure from the land, in triumph to the capital. Montezuma offered to support him with five thousand Aztec warriors; but the general declined it, not choosing to encumber himself with a body of doubtful, perhaps disaffected, auxiliaries.

He left in garrison, under Alvarado, one hundred and forty men, two thirds of his whole force. With these remained all the artillery, the greater part of the little body of horse, and most of the arquebusiers. He took with him only seventy soldiers, but they were men of the most mettle in the army and his stanch adherents. They were lightly armed and encumbered with as little baggage as possible. Every thing depended on celerity of movement.

Montezuma, in his royal litter borne on the shoulders of his nobles, and escorted by the whole Spanish infantry, accompanied the general to the causeway. There, embracing him in the most cordial manner, they parted, with all the external marks of mutual regard. – It was about the middle of May, 1520, more than six months since the entrance of the Spanish to Mexico. During this time they had lorded it over the land with absolute sway. They were now leaving the city in hostile array, not against an Indian foe, but their own countrymen. It was the beginning of a long career of calamity, – chequered, indeed, by occasional triumphs, – which was yet to be run before the Conquest could be completed.

Traversing the southern causeway, by which they had entered the capital, the little party were soon on their march across the beautiful Valley. They climbed the mountain screen which Nature had so ineffectually drawn around it; passed between the huge volcanoes that, like faithless watch-dogs on their posts, have long since been buried in slumber; threaded the intricate defiles where they had before experienced such bleak and tempestuous weather; and, emerging on the other side, descended the western slope which opens on the wide expanse of the fruitful plateau of Cholula.

They heeded little of what they saw on their rapid march, nor whether it was cold or hot. The anxiety of their minds made them indifferent to outward annoyances; and they had fortunately none to encounter from the natives, for the name of Spaniard was in itself a charm, – a better guard than helm or buckler to the bearer.

In Cholula, Cortés had the inexpressible satisfaction of meeting Velasquez de Leon, with the hundred and twenty soldiers intrusted to his command for the formation of a colony. That faithful officer had been some time at Cholula, waiting for the general's approach. Had he failed, the enterprise of Cortés must have failed also. The idea of resistance, with his own handful of followers, would have been chimerical. As it was, his little band was now trebled, and acquired a confidence in proportion.

Cordially embracing their companions in arms, now knit together more closely than ever by the sense of a great and common danger, the combined troops traversed with quick step the streets of the sacred city, where many a dark pile of ruins told of their disastrous visit on the preceding autumn. They kept the high road to Tlascala; and, at not many leagues' distance from the capital, fell in with father Olmedo and his companions on their return from the camp of Narvaez, to which, it will be remembered, they had been sent as envoys. The ecclesiastic bore a letter from that commander, in which he summoned Cortés and his followers to submit to his authority as captain general of the country, menacing them with condign punishment, in case of refusal or delay. Olmedo gave many curious particulars of the state of the enemy's camp. Narvaez he described as puffed up by authority, and negligent of precautions against a foe whom he held in contempt. He was surrounded by a number of pompous conceited officers, who ministered to his vanity, and whose braggart tones, the good father, who had an eye for the ridiculous, imitated, to the no small diversion of Cortés and the soldiers. Many of the troops, he said, showed no great partiality for their commander, and were strongly disinclined to a rupture with their countrymen; a state of feeling much promoted by the accounts they had received of Cortés, by his own arguments and promises, and by the liberal distribution of the gold with which he had been provided. In addition to these matters, Cortés gathered much important intelligence respecting the position of the enemy's force, and his general plan of operations.

At Tlascala, the Spaniards were received with a frank and friendly hospitality. It is not said, whether any of the Tlascalan allies had accompanied them from Mexico. If they did, they went no further than their native city. Cortés requested a reinforcement of six hundred fresh troops to attend him on his present expedition. It was readily granted; but, before the army had proceed many miles on its route, the Indian auxiliaries fell off, one after another, and returned to their city. They had no personal feeling of animosity to gratify in the present instance, as in a war against Mexico. It may be, too, that, although intrepid in a contest with the bravest of the Indian races, they had had too fatal experience of the prowess of the white men, to care to measure swords with them again. At any rate, they deserted in such numbers, that Cortés dismissed the remainder at once, saying, good-humoredly, "He had rather part with them then, than in the hour of trial."

The troops soon entered on that wild district in the neighbourhood of Perote, strewed with the wreck of volcanic matter, which forms so singular a contrast to the general character of beauty with which the scenery is stamped. It was not long before their eyes were gladdened by the approach of Sandoval and about sixty soldiers from the garrison of Vera Cruz, including several deserters from the enemy. It was a most important reinforcement, not more on account of the numbers of the men than of the character of the commander, in every respect one of the ablest captains in the service. He had been compelled to fetch a circuit, in order to avoid failing in with the enemy, and had forced his way through thick forests and wild mountain passes, till he had fortunately, without accident, reached the appointed place of rendezvous, and stationed himself once more under the banner of his chieftain.

At the same place, also, Cortés was met by Tobillos, a Spaniard whom he had sent to procure the lances from Chinantla. They were perfectly well made, after the pattern which had been given; double-headed spears, tipped with copper, and of great length. Tobillos drilled the men in the exercise of this weapon, the formidable uses of which, especially against horse, had been fully demonstrated, towards the close of the last century, by the Swiss battalions, in their encounters with the Burgundian chivalry, the best in Europe.

Cortés now took a review of his army, – if so paltry a force may be called an army, – and found their numbers were two hundred and sixty-six, only five of whom were mounted. A few muskets and cross-bows were sprinkled among them. In defensive armor they were sadly deficient. They were for the most part cased in the quilted doublet of the country, thickly stuffed with cotton, the *escaupil*, recommended by its superior lightness, but which, though competent to turn the arrow of the Indian, was ineffectual against a musket-ball. Most of this cotton mail was exceedingly out of repair, giving evidence, in its unsightly gaps, of much rude service, and hard blows. Few, in this emergency, but would have given almost any price – the best of the gold chains which they wore in tawdry display over their poor habiliments – for a steel morion or cuirass, to take the place of their own hacked and battered armor.

Under this course covering, however, they bore hearts stout and courageous as ever beat in human bosoms. For they were the heroes, still invincible, of many a hard-fought field, where the odds had been incalculably against them. They had large experience of the country and of the natives; knew well the character of their own commander, under whose eye they had been trained, till every movement was in obedience to him. The whole body seemed to constitute but a single individual, in respect of unity of design and of action. Thus its real effective force was incredibly augmented; and, what was no less important, the humblest soldier felt it to be so.

The troops now resumed their march across the table-land, until reaching the western slope, their labors were lightened, as they descended towards the broad plains of the *tierra caliente*, spread out like a boundless ocean of verdure below them. At some fifteen leagues' distance from Cempoalla, where Narvaez had established his quarters, they were met by another embassy from that commander. It consisted of the priest, Guevara, Andres de Duero, and two or three others. Duero, the fast friend of Cortés, had been the person most instrumental, originally, in obtaining him his commission from Velasquez. They now greeted each other with a warm embrace, and it was not till after much preliminary conversation on private matters, that the secretary disclosed the object of his visit.

He bore a letter from Narvaez, couched in terms somewhat different from the preceding. That officer required, indeed, the acknowledgment of his paramount authority in the land, but offered his vessels to transport all who desired it, from the country, together with their treasures and effects, without molestation or inquiry. The more liberal tenor of these terms was, doubtless, to be ascribed to the influence of Duero. The secretary strongly urged Cortés to comply with them, as the most favorable that could be obtained, and as the only alternative affording him a chance of safety in his desperate condition. "For, however valiant your men may be, how can they expect," he asked, "to face a force so much superior in numbers and equipment as that of their antagonist?" But Cortés had set his fortunes on the cast, and he was not the man to shrink from it. "If Narvaez bears a royal commission," he returned, "I will readily submit to him. But he has produced none. He is a deputy of my rival,

94

Velasquez. For myself, I am a servant of the king, I have conquered the country for him; and for him I and my brave followers will defend it, be assured, to the last drop of our blood. If we fall it will be glory enough to have perished in the discharge of our duty."

His friend might have been somewhat puzzled to comprehend how the authority of Cortés rested on a different ground from that of Narvaez; and if they both held of the same superior, the governor of Cuba, why that dignitary should not be empowered to supersede his own officer in case of dissatisfaction, and appoint a substitute. But Cortés here reaped the full benefit of that legal fiction, if it may be so termed, by which his commission, resigned to the self-constituted municipality of Vera Cruz, was again derived through that body from the Crown. The device, indeed was too palpable to impose on any but those who chose to be blinded. Most of the army were of this number. To them it seemed to give additional confidence, in the same manner as a strip of painted canvass, when substituted, as it has sometimes been, for a real parapet of stone, has been found not merely to impose on the enemy, but to give a sort of artificial courage to the defenders concealed behind it.

Duero had arranged with his friend in Cuba, when he took command of the expedition, that he himself was to have a liberal share of the profits. It is said that Cortés confirmed this arrangement at the present juncture, and made it clearly for the other's interest that he should prevail in the struggle with Narvaez. This was an important point, considering the position of the secretary. From this authentic source the general derived much information respecting the designs of Narvaez, which had escaped the knowledge of Olmedo.

On the departure of the envoys, Cortés intrusted them with a letter for his rival, a counterpart of that which he had received from him. This show of negotiation intimated a desire on his part to postpone, if not avoid hostilities, which might the better put Narvaez off his guard. In the letter he summoned that commander and his followers to present themselves before him without delay, and to acknowledge his authority as the representative of his sovereign. He should otherwise be compelled to proceed against them as rebels to the Crown! With this missive, the vaunting tone of which was intended quite as much for his own troops as the enemy, Cortés dismissed the envoys. They returned to disseminate among their comrades their admiration of the general, and of his unbounded liberality, of which he took care they should experience full measure, and they dilated on the riches of his adherents, who, over their wretched attire, displayed with ostentatious profusion, jewels, ornaments of gold, collars, and massive chains winding several times round their necks and bodies, the rich spoil of the treasury of Montezuma.

The army now took its way across the level plains of the *tierra caliente*, on which nature has exhausted all the wonders of creation; it was covered more thickly then, than in the present day, with noble forests, where the towering cotton-wood tree, the growth of ages, stood side by side with the light bamboo, or banana, the product of a season, each in its way attesting the marvellous fecundity of the soil, while innumerable creeping flowers, muffling up the giant branches of the trees, waved in bright festoons above their heads, loading the air with odors. But the senses of the Spaniards were not open to the delicious influences of nature. Their minds were occupied by one idea.

Cortés announced his purpose to attack the enemy that very night, when he should be buried in slumber, and the friendly darkness might throw a veil over their own movements, and conceal the poverty of their numbers. To this the troops, jaded though they were by incessant marching, and half famished, joyfully assented. In their situation, suspense was the worst of evils. He next distributed the commands among his captains. To Gonzalo de Sandoval he assigned the important office of taking Narvaez. He was commanded, as *alguacil mayor*, to seize the person of that officer as a rebel to his sovereign, and, if he made resistance, to kill him on the spot. He was provided with sixty picked men to aid him in this difficult task, supported by several of the ablest captains, among whom were two of the Alvarados, de Avila, and Ordaz. The largest division of the force was placed under Christoval de Olid, or, according to some authorities, of Pizarro, one of that family so renowned in the subsequent conquest of Peru. He was to get possession of the artillery, and to cover the assault of Sandoval by keeping those of the enemy at bay, who would interfere with it. Cortés reserved only a body of twenty men for himself, to act on any point that occasion might require. The watch-word was *Espíritu Santo*, it being the evening of Whitsunday. Having made these arrangements, he prepared to cross the river.

During the interval thus occupied by Cortés, Narvaez had remained at Cempoalla, passing his days in idle and frivolous amusement. From this he was at length roused, after the return of Duero, by the remonstrances of the old cacique of the city. "Why are you so heedless?" exclaimed the latter; "do you think Malintzin is so? Depend on it, he knows your situation exactly, and, when you least dream of it, he will be upon you."

Alarmed at these suggestions and those of his friends, Narvaez at length put himself at the head of his troops, and, on the very day on which Cortés arrived at the River of Canoes, sallied out to meet him. But, when he had reached this barrier, Narvaez saw no sign of the enemy. The rain, which fell in torrents, soon drenched the soldiers to the skin. Made somewhat effeminate by their long and luxurious residence at Cempoalla, they murmured at their uncomfortable situation. "Of what use was it to remain there fighting with the elements? There was no sign of an enemy, and little reason to apprehend his approach in such tempestuous weather. It would be wiser to return to Cempoalla, and in the morning they should be all fresh for action, should Cortés make his appearance."

Narvaez took counsel of these advisors, or rather of his own inclinations. Before retracing his steps, he provided against surprise, by stationing a couple of sentinels at no great distance from the river, to give notice of the approach of Cortés. He also detached a body of forty horse in another direction, by which he thought it not improbable the enemy might advance on Cempoalla. Having taken these precautions, he fell back again before night on his own quarters and soon after to repose, with as much indifference as if his rival had been on the other side of the Atlantic, instead of a neighbouring stream.

That stream was now converted by the deluge of waters into a furious torrent. It was with difficulty that a practicable ford could be found. The slippery stones, rolling beneath the feet, gave way at every step. The difficulty of the passage was much increased by the darkness and driving tempest. Still, with their long pikes, the Spaniards contrived to make good their footing, at least, all but two, who were swept down by the fury of the current. When they had reached the opposite side, they had new impediments to encounter in traversing a road, never good, now made double difficult by the deep mire, and the tangled brushwood with which it was overrun.

Here they met with a cross, which had been raised by them on their former march into the interior. They hailed it as a good omen; and Cortés, kneeling before the blessed sign, confessed his sins, and declared his great object to be the triumph of the holy Catholic faith. The army followed his example, and, having made a general confession, received absolution from father Olmedo, who invoked the blessing of Heaven on the warriors who had consecrated their swords to the glory of the Cross. Then rising up and embracing one another, as companions in the good cause, they found themselves wonderfully invigorated and refreshed.

Silently and stealthily they held on their way without beat of drum, or sound of trumpet, when they suddenly came on the two sentinels who had been stationed by Narvaez to give notice of their approach. This had been so noiseless, that the videttes were both of them surprised on their post, and one only, with difficulty, effected his escape. The other was brought before Cortés. Every effort was made to draw from him some account of the present position of Narvaez. But the man remained obstinately silent; and, though threatened with the gibbet, and having a noose actually drawn round his neck, his Spartan heroism was not to be vanquished. Fortunately no change had taken place in the arrangements of Narvaez since the intelligence previously derived from Duero.

The other sentinel, who had escaped, carried the news of the enemy's approach to the camp. But his report was not credited by the lazy soldiers, whose slumbers he had disturbed. "He had been decided by his fears," they said, "and mistaken the noise of the storm and the waving of the bushes, for the enemy. Cortés and his men were far enough on the other side of the river, which they would be slow to cross in such a night." Narvaez himself shared in the same blind infatuation, and the discredited sentinel slunk abashed to his own quarters, vainly menacing them with the consequences of their incredulity.

Cortés, not doubting that the sentinel's report must alarm the enemy's camp, quickened his pace. As he drew near, he discerned a light in one of the lofty towers of the city. "It is the quarters of Narvaez," he exclaimed to Sandoval, "and that light must be your beacon." On entering the suburbs, the Spaniards were surprised to find no one stirring, and no symptom of alarm. Not a sound was to be heard, except the measured tread of their own footsteps, half-drowned in the howling of the tempest. Still they could not move so stealthily as altogether to elude notice, as they defiled through the streets of this populous city. The tidings were quickly conveyed to the enemy's quarters, where, in an instant, all was bustle and confusion. The trumpets sounded to arms. The dragoons sprang to their steeds, the artillerymen to their guns. Narvaez hastily buckled on his armor, called his men around him, and summoned those in the neighbouring *teocallis* to join him in the area. He gave his orders with coolness; for, however wanting in prudence, he was not deficient in presence of mind or courage.

All this was the work of a few minutes. But in those

minutes the Spaniards had reached the avenue leading to the camp. Cortés ordered his men to keep close to the walls of the buildings, that the cannon-shot might have a free range. No sooner had they presented themselves before the inclosure, than the artillery of Narvaez opened a general fire. Fortunately the pieces were pointed so high that most of the balls passed over their heads, and three men only were struck down. They did not give the enemy time to reload. Cortés shouting the watchword of the night, "Espíritu Santo! Espíritu Santo! Upon them!" in a moment Olid and his division rushed on the artillerymen, whom they pierced, or knocked down with their pikes, and got possession of their guns. Another division engaged the cavalry, and made a diversion in favor of Sandoval, who with his gallant little band sprang up the great stairway of the temple. They were received with a shower of missiles, – arrows, and musket-balls, which, in the hurried aim, and the darkness of the night, did little mischief. The next minute the assailants were on the platform, engaged hand to hand with their foes. Narvaez fought bravely in the midst, encouraging his followers. His standard-bearer fell by his side, run through the body. He himself received several wounds; for his short sword was no match for the long pikes of the assailants. At length, he received a blow from a spear, which struck out his left eye. "Santa María!" exclaimed the unhappy man, "I am slain!" The cry was instantly taken up by the followers of Cortés, who shouted, "Victory!"

Disabled, and half mad with agony, from his wound, Narvaez was withdrawn by his men into the sanctuary. The assailants endeavoured to force an entrance, but it was stoutly defended. At length a soldier, getting possession of a torch, or firebrand, flung it on the thatched roof, and in a few moments the combustible materials of which it was composed were in a blaze. Those within were driven out by the suffocating heat and smoke. A soldier named Farfan grappled with the wounded commander, and easily brought him to the ground; when he was speedily dragged down the steps, and secured with fetters. His followers, seeing the fate of their chief, made no further resistance.

During this time Cortés and the troops of Olid had been engaged with the cavalry, and had discomfited them, after some ineffectual attempts on the part of the latter to break through the dense array of pikes, by which several of their number were unhorsed and some of them slain. The general then prepared to assault the other *teocallis*, first summoning the garrisons to surrender. As they refused, he brought up the heavy guns to bear on them, thus turning the artillery against its own masters. He accompanied this menacing movement with offers of the most liberal import; an amnesty of the past, and a full participation in all the advantages of the Conquest. The garrison waited only for one discharge of the ordnance, when they accepted the terms of capitulation.

The number of the slain is variously reported. It seems probably that not more than twelve perished on the side of the vanquished, and of the victors half that number. The small amount may be explained by the short duration of the action, and the random aim of the missiles in the darkness. The number of the wounded was much more considerable.

The field was now completely won. A few brief hours had sufficed to change the condition of Cortés from that of a wandering outlaw at the head of a handful of needy adventurers, a rebel with a price upon his head, to that of an independent chief, with a force at his disposal strong enough not only to secure his present conquests, but to open a career for still loftier ambition. While the air rung with the acclamations of the soldiery, the victorious general, assuming a deportment corresponding with his change of fortune, took his seat in the chair of state, and, with a rich embroidered mantle thrown over his shoulder, received, one by one, the officers and soldiers, as they came to tender their congratulations. The privates were graciously permitted to kiss his hand. The officers he noticed with words of compliment or courtesy; and, when Duero, Bermudez the treasurer, and some others of the vanquished party, his old friends, presented themselves, he cordially embraced them.

Narvaez, Salvatierra, and two or three of the hostile leaders were led before him in chains. It was a moment of deep humiliation for the former commander, in which the anguish of the body, however keen, must be forgotten in that of the spirit. "You have great reason, Señor Cortés," said the discomfited warrior, "to thank Fortune for having given you the day so easily, and put me in your power." – "I have much to be thankful for," replied the general; "but for my victory over you, I esteem it as one of the least of my achievements since my coming into the country!" He then ordered the wounds of the prisoners to be cared for, and sent them under a strong guard to Vera Cruz.

Notwithstanding the proud humility of his reply, Cortés could scarcely have failed to regard his victory over Narvaez as one of the most brilliant achievements in his career. With a few scores of followers, badly clothed, worse fed, wasted by forced marches, under every personal disadvantage, deficient in weapons and military stores, he had attacked in their own quarter, routed, and captured the entire force of the enemy, thrice his superior in numbers, well provided with cavalry and artillery, admirably equipped, and complete in all the munitions of war! The amount of troops engaged on either side was, indeed, inconsiderable. But the proportions are not affected by this: and the relative strength of the parties made a result so decisive one of the most remarkable events in the annals of war.

The city was in a state of insurrection. No sooner had the struggle with his rival been decided than Cortés dispatched a courier with the tidings to the capital. In less than a fortnight, the same messenger returned with letters for Alvarado, conveying the alarming information, that the Mexicans were in arms, and had vigorously assaulted the Spaniards in their own quarters. The enemy, he added, had burned the brigantines, by which Cortés had secured the means of retreat in case of the destruction of the bridges. They had attempted to force the defences, and had succeeded in partially undermining them, and they had overwhelmed the garrison with a tempest of missiles, which had killed several, and wounded a great number. The letter concluded with beseeching his commander to hasten to their relief, if he would save them, or keep his hold on the capital.

These tidings were a heavy blow to the general, – the heavier, it seemed, coming, as they did, in the hour of triumph, when he had thought to have all his enemies at his feet. There was no room for hesitation. To lose their footing in the capital, the noblest city in the Western World, would be to lose the country itself, which looked up to it as its head. He opened the matter fully to his soldiers, calling on all who would save their countrymen to follow him. All declared their readiness to go; showing an alacrity, says Diaz, which some would have been slow to manifest, had they foreseen the future.

Cortés now made preparations for instant departure. Nothing worthy of notice occurred during the first part of the march. The troops everywhere met with a friendly reception from the peasantry, who readily supplied their wants. Some time before reaching Tlascala, the route lay through a country thinly settled, and the army experienced considerable suffering from want of food, and still more from that of water. Their distress increased to an alarming degree, as, in the hurry of their forced march, they travelled with the meridian sun beating fiercely on their heads. Several faltered by the way, and, throwing themselves down by the road-side, seemed incapable of further effort, and almost indifferent to life.

As they descended into the populous plains, their reception by the natives was very different from that which they had experienced on the preceding visit. There were no groups of curious peasantry to be seen gazing at them as they passed, and offering their simple hospitality. The supplies they asked were not refused, but granted with an ungracious air, that showed the blessing of the giver did not accompany them. This air of reserve became still more marked as the army entered the suburbs of the ancient capital of the Acolhuans. No one came forth to greet them, and the population seemed to have dwindled away, – so many of them were withdrawn to the neighbouring scene of hostilities at Mexico. Their cold reception was a sensible mortification to the veterans of Cortés, who, judging from the past, had boasted to their new comrades of the sensation their presence would excite among the natives. The cacique of the place, who, as it may be remembered, had been created through the influence of Cortés, was himself absent. The general drew an ill omen from all these circumstances, which even raised an uncomfortable apprehension in his mind respecting the fate of the garrison in Mexico.

But his doubts were soon dispelled by the arrival of a messenger in a canoe from that city, whence he had escaped through the remissness of the enemy, or, perhaps, with their connivance. He brought dispatches from Alvarado, informing his commander that the Mexicans had for the last fortnight desisted from active hostilities and converted their operations into a blockade. The garrison had suffered greatly, but Alvarado expressed his conviction that the siege would be raised, and tranquillity restored, on the approach of his countrymen. Montezuma sent a messenger, also, to the same effect. At the same time, he exculpated himself from any part in the late hostilities, which he said had not only been conducted without his privity, but contrary to his inclination and efforts.

The Spanish general, having halted long enough to refresh his wearied troops, took up his march along the southern margin of the lake, which led him over the same causeway by which he had before entered the capital. It was the day consecrated to St. John the Baptist, the 24th of June, 1520. But how different was the scene from that presented on his former entrance! No crowds now lined the roads, no boats swarmed on the lake, filled with admiring spectators. A single pirogue might now and then be seen in the distance, like a spy stealthily watching their movements, and darting away the moment it had attracted notice. A death-like stillness brooded over the scene, – a stillness that spoke louder to the heart, than the acclamations of multitudes.

Cortés rode on moodily at the head of his battalions, finding abundant food for meditation, doubtless, in this change of circumstances. As if to dispel these gloomy reflections, he ordered his trumpets to sound, and their clear, shrill notes, borne across the waters, told the inhabitants of the beleaguered fortress, that their friends were at hand. They were answered by a joyous peal of artillery, which seemed to give a momentary exhilaration to the troops, as they quickened their pace, traversed the great draw-bridges, and once more found themselves within the walls of the imperial city.

The appearance of things here was not such as to allay their apprehensions. In some places they beheld the smaller bridges removed, intimating too plainly, now that their brigantines were destroyed, how easy it would be to cut off their retreat. The town seemed even more deserted than Tezcuco. Its once busy and crowded population had mysteriously vanished. And, as the Spaniards defiled through the empty streets, the tramp of their horses' feet upon the pavement was answered by dull and melancholy echoes that fell heavily on their hearts. With saddened feelings they reached the great gates of the palace of Axayacatl. The gates were thrown open, and Cortés and his veterans, rushing in, were cordially embraced by their companions in arms, while both parties soon forgot the present in the interesting recapitulation of the past.

The first inquiries of the general were respecting the origin of the tumult. The accounts were various. Some imputed it to the desire of the Mexicans to release their sovereign from confinement; others to the design of cutting off the garrison while crippled by the absence of Cortés and their countrymen. All agreed, however, in tracing the immediate cause to the violence of Alvarado. It was common for the Aztecs to celebrate an annual festival in May, in honor of their patron war-god. It was called the "incensing of Huitzilopotchli," and was commemorated by sacrifice, religious songs, and dances, in which most of the nobles engaged, for it was one of the great festivals which displayed the pomp of the Aztec ritual. As it was held in the court of the *teocalli*, in the immediate neighbourhood of the Spanish quarters, and as a part of the temple itself was reserved for a Christian chapel, the caciques asked permission of Alvarado to perform their rites there. They requested also, it is said, to be allowed the presence of Montezuma. This latter petition Alvarado declined, in obedience to the injunctions of Cortés; but acquiesced in the former, on condition that the Aztecs should celebrate no human sacrifices, and should come without weapons.

They assembled accordingly on the day appointed, to the number of six hundred, at the smallest computation. They were dressed in their most magnificent gala costumes, with their graceful mantles of feather-work, sprinkled with precious stones, and their necks, arms, and legs ornamented with collars and bracelets of gold. They had that love of gaudy splendor which belongs to semi-civilized nations, and on these occasions displayed all the pomp and profusion of their barbaric wardrobes.

Alvarado and his soldiers attended as spectators, some of them taking their station at the gates, as if by chance, and others mingling in the crowd. They were all armed, a circumstance, which, as it was usual, excited no attention. The Aztecs were soon engrossed by the exciting movement of the dance, accompanied by their religious chant and wild, discordant minstrelsy. While thus occupied, Alvarado and his men, at a concerted signal, rushed with drawn swords on their victims. Unprotected by armor or weapons of any kind, they were hewn down without resistance by their assailants, who, in their bloody work, says a contemporary, showed no touch of pity or compunction. Some fled to the gates, but were caught on the long pikes of the soldiers. Others, who attempted to scale the *Coatepantli*, or Wall of Serpents, as it was called, which surrounded the area, shared the like fate, or were cut to pieces, or shot by the ruthless soldiery. The pavement, says a writer of the age, ran with streams of blood, like water in a heavy shower. Not an Aztec, of all that gay company, was left alive! It was repeating the dreadful scene of Cholula, with the disgraceful addition, that the Spaniards, not content with slaughtering their victims, rifled them of the precious ornaments on their persons! On this sad day fell the flower of the Aztec nobility. Not a family of note, but had mourning and desolation brought within its walls. And many a doleful ballad, rehearsing the tragic incidents of the story, and adapted to the plaintive national airs, continued to be chanted by the natives long after the subjugation of the country.

No sooner was the butchery accomplished, than the tidings spread like wildfire through the capital. Men could scarcely credit their senses. All they had hitherto suffered, the desecration of their temples, the imprisonment of their sovereign, the insults heaped on his person, all were forgotten in this one act. Every feeling of long smothered hostility and rancor now burst forth in the cry for vengeance. Every former sentiment of superstitious dread was merged in that of inextinguishable hatred. It required no effort of the priests – though this was not wanting – to fan these passions into a blaze. The city rose in arms to a man; and on the following dawn, almost before the Spaniards could secure themselves in their defences, they were assaulted with desperate fury. Some of the assailants attempted to scale the walls; others succeeded in partially undermining and in setting fire to the works. Whether they would have succeeded in carrying the place by storm is doubtful. But, at the prayers of the garrison, Montezuma himself interfered, and mounting the battlements addressed the populace, whose fury he endeavoured to mitigate by urging considerations for his own safety. They respected their monarch so far as to desist from further attempts to storm the fortress, but changed their operations into a regular blockade. They threw up works around the palace to prevent the egress of the Spaniards. They suspended the *tianguez*, or market, to preclude the possibility of their enemy's obtaining supplies; and they then quietly sat down, with feelings of sullen desperation, waiting for the hour when famine should throw their victims into their hands.

The condition of the besieged, meanwhile, was sufficiently distressing. Their magazines of provisions, it is true, were not exhausted; but they suffered greatly from want of water, which, within the inclosure, was exceedingly brackish, for the soil was saturated with the salt of the surrounding element. In this extremity, they discovered, it is said, a spring of fresh water in the area. Such springs were known in some other parts of the city; but, discovered first under these circumstances, it was accounted as nothing less than a miracle. Still they suffered much from their past encounters. Seven Spaniards, and many Tlascalans, had fallen, and there was scarcely one of either nation who had not received several wounds. In this situation, far from their own countrymen, without expectation of succour from abroad, they seemed to have no alternative before them, but a lingering death by famine, or one more dreadful on the altar of sacrifice. From this gloomy state they were relieved by the coming of their comrades.

On the day Cortés arrived, Montezuma had left his own quarters to welcome him. But the Spanish commander, distrusting, as it would seem, however reasonably, his good faith, received him so coldly that the Indian monarch withdrew, displeased and dejected, to his own apartment. As the Mexican populace made no show of submission, and brought no supplies to the army, the general's ill-humor with the emperor continued. When, therefore, Montezuma sent some of the nobles to ask an interview with Cortés, the latter, turning to his own officers, haughtily exclaimed, "What have I to do with this dog of a king who suffers us to starve before his eyes?"

His captains, among whom were Olid, de Avila, and Velasquez de Leon, endeavoured to mitigate his anger, reminding him, in respectful terms, that, had it not been for the emperor, the garrison might even now have been overwhelmed by the enemy. This remonstrance only chafed him the more. "Did not the dog," he asked, repeating the opprobrious epithet, "betray us in his communications with Narvaez? And does he not now suffer his markets to be

111

closed, and leave us to die of famine?" Then, turning fiercely to the Mexicans, he said, "Go, tell your master and his people to open the markets, or we will do it for them, at their cost!" The chiefs, who had gathered the import of his previous taunt on their sovereign, from his tone and gesture, or perhaps from some comprehension of his language, left his presence swelling with resentment; and, in communicating his message, took care it should lose none of its effect.

Shortly after, Cortés, at the suggestion, it is said, of Montezuma, released his brother Cuitlahua, lord of Iztapalapan, who had been seized on suspicion of coöperating with the chief of Tezcuco in his meditated revolt. It was thought he might be of service in allaying the present tumult, and bringing the populace to a better state of feeling. But he returned no more to the fortress. He was a bold, ambitious prince, and the injuries he had received from the Spaniards rankled deep in his bosom. He was presumptive heir to the crown, which, by the Aztec laws of succession, descended much more frequently in a collateral than in a direct line. The people welcomed him as the representative of their sovereign, and chose him to supply the place of Montezuma during his captivity. Cuitlahua willingly accepted the post of honor and of danger. He was an experienced warrior, and exerted himself to reorganize the disorderly levies, and to arrange a more efficient plan of operations. The effect was soon visible.

Cortés, meanwhile had so little doubt of his ability to overawe the insurgents, that he wrote to that effect to the garrison of Villa Rica, by the same dispatches in which he informed them of his safe arrival in the capital. But scarcely had his messenger been gone half an hour, when he returned breathless with terror, and covered with wounds. "The city," he said, "was all in arms! The drawbridges were raised, and the enemy would soon be upon them!" He spoke truth. It was not long before a hoarse, sullen sound became audible, like that of the roaring of distant waters. It grew louder and louder; till, from the parapet surrounding the inclosure, the great avenues which led to it might be seen dark with the masses of warriors, who came rolling on in a confused tide towards the fortress. At the same time, the terraces and *azoteas* or flat roofs, in the neighbourhood, were thronged with combatants brandishing their missiles, who seemed to have risen up as if by magic! It was a spectacle to appal the stoutest.

The fight now raged with fury on both sides. The walls around the palace belched forth an unintermitting sheet of flame and smoke. The groans of the wounded and dying were lost in the fiercer battle-cries of the combatants, the roar of the artillery, the sharper rattle of the musketry, and the hissing sound of Indian missiles. It was the conflict of the European with the American; of civilized man with the barbarian; of the science of the one with the rude weapons and warfare of the other. And as the ancient walls of Tenochtitlan shook under the thunders of the artillery, – it announced that the white man, the destroyer, had set his foot within her precincts.

Night at length came, and drew her friendly mantle over the contest. The Aztec seldom fought by night. It brought little repose, however, to the Spaniards, in hourly expectation of an assault; and they found abundant occupation in restoring the breaches in their defences, and in repairing their battered armor. The beleaguering host lay on their arms through the night, giving token of their presence, now and then, by sending a stone or shaft over the battlements, or by a solitary cry of defiance from some warrior more determined than the rest, till all other sounds were lost in the vague, indistinct murmurs which float upon the air in the neighbourhood of a vast assembly.

With early dawn, the Spaniards were up and under arms; but not before their enemies had given evidence of their hostility by the random missiles, which, from time to time, were sent into the enclosure. As the grey light of morning advanced, it showed the besieging army far from being diminished in numbers, filling up the great square and neighbouring avenues in more dense array than on the preceding evening. Instead of a confused, disorderly rabble, it had the appearance of something like a regular force, with its battalions distributed under their respective banners, the devices of which showed a contribution from the principal cities and districts in the Valley. High above the rest was conspicuous the ancient standard of Mexico, with its well-known cognizance, an eagle pouncing on an ocelot, emblazoned on a rich mantle of featherwork. Here and there priest might be seen mingling in the ranks of the besiegers, and with frantic gestures, animating them to avenge their insulted deities.

Cortés suffered much from a severe wound which he had received in the hand in the late action. But the anguish of his mind must have been still greater, as he brooded over the dark prospect before him. He had mistaken the character of the Mexicans. Their long and patient endurance had been a violence to their natural temper, which, as their whole history proves, was arrogant and ferocious beyond that of most of the races of Anahuac. The restraint, which, in deference to their monarch, more than to their own fears, they had so long put on their natures, being once removed, their passions burst forth with accumulated violence. The Spaniards had encountered in the Tlascalan an open enemy, who had no grievance to complain of, no wrong to redress. He fought under the vague apprehension only of some coming evil to his country. But the Aztec hitherto the proud lord of the land, was goaded by insult and injury, till he had reached that pitch of self-devotion, which made life cheap, in comparison with revenge. Armed thus with the energy of despair, the savage is almost a match for the civilized man; and a whole nation, moved to its depths by a common feeling, which swallows up all selfish considerations of personal interest and safety, becomes, whatever be its resources, like the earthquake and the tornado, the most formidable among the agencies of nature.

Considerations of this kind may have passed through the mind of Cortés, as he reflected on his own impotence to restrain the fury of the Mexicans, and resolved, in despite of his late supercilious treatment of Montezuma, to employ his authority to allay the tumult.

Cortés now sent to the Aztec emperor to request his interposition with his subjects in behalf of the Spaniards. But Montezuma was not in the humor to comply. He had remained moodily in his quarters ever since the general's return. Disgusted with the treatment he had received, he had still further cause for mortification in finding himself the ally of those who were the open enemies of his nation. On being assured, however, that the Spaniards would willingly depart, if a way were opened to them by their enemies, he at length – moved, probably, more by the desire to spare the blood of his subjects, than of the Christians – consented to expostulate with his people.

In order to give the greater effect to his presence, he put on his imperial robes. The *tilmatli*, his mantle of white and blue, flowed over his shoulders, held together by its rich clasp of the green *chalchivitl*. The same precious gem, with emeralds of uncommon size, set in gold, profusely ornamented with other parts of his dress. His feet were shod with the golden sandals, and his brows covered by the *copilli*, or Mexican diadem, resembling in form the pontifical tiara. Thus attired, and surrounded by a guard of Spaniards and several Aztec nobles, and preceded by the golden wand, the symbol of sovereignty, the Indian monarch ascended the central turret of the palace. His presence was instantly recognised by the people, and, as the royal retinue advanced along the battlements, a change, as if by magic, came over the scene. The clang of instruments, the fierce cries of the assailants, were hushed, and a death-like stillness pervaded the whole assembly, so fiercely agitated, but a few moments before, by the wild tumult of war! Many prostrated themselves on the ground; others bent the knee; and all turned with eager expectation towards the monarch, whom they had been taught to reverence with slavish awe, and from whose countenance they had been wont to turn away as from the intolerable splendors of divinity! Montezuma saw his advantage; and while he stood thus confronted with his awe-struck people, he seemed to recover all his former authority and confidence, as he felt himself to be still a king. With a calm voice, easily heard over the silent assembly, he is said by the Castilian writers to have thus addressed them.

"Why do I see my people here in arms against the palace of my fathers? Is it that you think your sovereign a prisoner, and wish to release him? If so, you have acted rightly. But you are mistaken. I am no prisoner. The strangers are my guests. I remain with them only from choice, and can leave them when I list. Have you come to drive them from the city? That is unnecessary. They will depart of their own accord, if you will open a way for them. Return to your homes, then. Lay down your arms. Show your obedience to me who have a right to it. The white men shall go back to their own land; and all shall be well again within the walls of Tenochtitlan."

As Montezuma announced himself the friend of the detested strangers, a murmur ran through the multitude; a murmur of contempt for the pusillanimous prince who could show himself so insensible to the insults and injuries for which the nation was in arms! The swollen tide of their passions swept away all the barriers of ancient reverence, and, taking a new direction, descended on the head of the unfortunate monarch, so far degenerated from his warlike ancestors.

"Base Aztec," they exclaimed, "woman, coward, the white men have made you a woman, – fit only to weave and spin!" These bitter taunts were soon followed by still more hostile demonstrations. A chief, it is said, of high rank, bent a bow or brandished a javelin with an air of defiance against the emperor, when, in an instant, a cloud of stones and arrows descended on the spot where the royal train was gathered. The Spaniards appointed to protect his person had been thrown off their guard by the respectful deportment of the people during their lord's address. They now hastily interposed their bucklers. But it was too late. Montezuma was wounded by three of the missiles, one of which, a stone, fell with such violence on his head, near the temple, as brought him senseless to the ground. The Mexicans, shocked at their own sacrilegious act, experienced a sudden revulsion of feeling, and, setting up a dismal cry, dispersed panic-struck, in different directions. Not one of the multitudinous array remained in the great square before the palace!

The unhappy prince, meanwhile, was borne by his attendants to his apartments below. On recovering from the insensibility caused by the blow, the wretchedness of his condition broke upon him. He had tasted the last bitterness of degradation. He had been reviled, rejected, by his people. The meanest of the rabble had raised their hands against him. He had nothing more to live for. It was in vain that Cortés and his officers endeavoured to soothe the anguish of his spirit and fill him with better thoughts. He spoke not a word in answer. His wound, though dangerous, might still, with skilful treatment, not prove mortal. But Montezuma refused all the remedies prescribed for it. He tore off the bandages as often as they were applied, maintaining all the while the most determined silence. He sat with eyes dejected, brooding over his fallen fortunes, over the image of ancient majesty and present humiliation. He had survived his honor. But a spark of his ancient spirit seemed to kindle in his bosom, as it was clear he did not mean to survive his disgrace. From this painful scene the Spanish general and his followers were soon called away by the new dangers which menaced the garrison.

Opposite to the Spanish quarters, at only a few rods' distance, stood the great *teocalli* of Huitzilopotchli. This pyramidal mound, with the sanctuaries that crowned it, rising altogether to a height of near a hundred and fifty feet, afforded an elevated position that completely commanded the palace of Axayacatl, occupied by the Christians. A body of five or six hundred Mexicans, many of them nobles and warriors of the highest rank, had got possession of the *teocalli*, whence they discharged such a tempest of arrows on the garrison, that no one could leave his defences for a moment without imminent danger; while the Mexicans, under shelter of the sanctuaries, were entirely covered from the fire of the besieged. It was obviously necessary to dislodge the enemy, if the Spaniards would remain longer in their quarters.

Cortés assigned this service to his chamberlain, Escobar, giving him a hundred men for the purpose, with orders to storm the *teocalli*, and set fire to the sanctuaries. But that officer was thrice repulsed in the attempt, and, after the most desperate efforts, was obliged to return with considerable loss, and without accomplishing his object.

Cortés, who saw the immediate necessity of carrying the place, determined to lead the storming party himself. He was then suffering much from the wound in his left hand, which had disabled it for the present. He made the arm serviceable, however, by fastening his buckler to it, and, thus crippled, sallied out at the head of three hundred chosen cavaliers, and several thousand of his auxiliaries.

In the court-yard of the temple he found a numerous body of Indians prepared to dispute his passage. He briskly charged them, but the flat, smooth stones of the pavement were so slippery, that the horses lost their footing, and many of them fell. Hastily dismounting, they sent back the animals to their quarters, and, renewing the assault, the Spaniards succeeded without much difficulty in dispersing the Indian warriors, and opening a free passage for themselves to the *teocalli*. This building, as the reader may remember, was a huge pyramidal structure, about three hundred feet square at the base. A flight of stone steps on the outside, at one of the angles of the mound, led to a platform, or terraced walk, which passed round the building until it reached a similar flight of stairs directly over the preceding, that conducted to another landing as before. As there were five bodies or divisions of the *teocalli*, it became necessary to pass round its whole extent four times, or nearly a mile, in order to reach the summit, which, it may be recollected, was an open area, crowned only by the two sanctuaries dedicated to the Aztec deities.

Cortés, having cleared a way for the assault, sprang up the lower stairway, followed by Alvarado, Sandoval, Ordaz, and the other gallant cavaliers of his little band, leaving a file of arquebusiers and a strong corps of Indian allies to hold the enemy in check at the foot of the monument. On the first landing, as well as on the several galleries above, and on the summit, the Aztec warriors were drawn up to dispute his passage. From their elevated position they showered down volleys of lighter missiles, together with heavy stones, beams, and burning rafters, which, thundering along the stairway, overturned the ascending Spaniards, and carried desolation through their ranks. The more fortunate, eluding or springing over these obstacles, succeeded in gaining the first terrace; where, throwing themselves on their enemies, they compelled them, after a short resistance, to fall back. The assailants pressed on, effectually supported by a brisk fire of the musketeers from below, which so much galled the Mexicans in their exposed situation, that they were glad to take shelter on the broad summit of the *teocalli*.

Cortés and his comrades were close upon their rear, and the two parties soon found themselves face to face on this aerial battle-field, engaged in mortal combat in presence of the whole city, as well as of the troops in the court-yard, who paused, as if by mutual consent, from their own hostilities, gazing in silent expectation on the issue of those above.

The parties closed with the desperate fury of men who had no hope but in victory. Quarter was neither asked nor given; and to fly was impossible. The edge of the area was unprotected by parapet or battlement. The least slip would be fatal; and the combatants, as they struggled in mortal agony, were sometimes seen to roll over the sheer sides of the precipice together. Cortés himself is said to have had a narrow escape from this dreadful fate. Two warriors, of strong, muscular frames, seized on him, and were dragging him violently towards the brink of the pyramid. Aware of their intention, he struggled with all his force, and, before they could accomplish their purpose, succeeded in tearing himself from their grasp, and hurling one of them over the walls with his own arm! The story is not improbable in itself, for Cortés was a man of uncommon agility and strength.

The battle lasted with unintermitting fury for three hours. The number of the enemy was double that of the Christians; and it seemed as if it were a contest which must be determined by numbers and brute force, rather than by superior science. But it was not so. The invulnerable armor of the Spaniard, his sword of matchless temper, and his skill in the use of it, gave him advantages which far outweighed the odds of physical strength and numbers. After doing all that the courage of despair could enable men to do, resistance grew fainter and fainter on the side of the Aztecs. One after another they had fallen. Two or three priests only survived to be led away in triumph by the victors. Every other combatant was stretched a corpse on the bloody arena, or had been hurled from the giddy heights. Yet the loss of the Spaniards was not inconsiderable. It amounted to forty-five of their best men, and nearly all the remainder were more or less injured in the desperate conflict.

Hoping to find the temper of the natives somewhat subdued by these reverses, Cortés now determined, with his usual policy, to make them a vantage-ground for proposing terms of accommodation. He accordingly invited the enemy to a parley, and, as the principal chiefs, attended by their followers, assembled in the great square, he mounted the turret before occupied by Montezuma and made signs that he would address them. Marina took her place by his side, as his interpreter. The multitude gazed with earnest curiosity on the Indian girl, whose influence with the Spaniards was well known, and whose connexion with the general, in particular, had led the Aztecs to designate him by her Mexican name of Malinche. Cortés speaking through the soft musical tones of his mistress, told his audience they must now be convinced, that they had nothing further to hope from opposition to the Spaniards. They had seen their gods trampled in the dust, their altars broken, the dwellings burned, their warriors falling on all sides. "All this," continued he, "you have brought on yourselves by your rebellion. Yet for the affection the sovereign, whom you have so unworthily treated, still bears you, I would willingly stay my hand, if you will lay down your arms, and return once more to your obedience. But, if you do not," he concluded, "I will make your city a heap of ruins, and leave not a soul alive to mourn over it!"

But the Spanish commander did not yet comprehend the character of the Aztecs, if he thought to intimidate them by menaces. Calm in their exterior and slow to move, they were the more difficult to pacify when roused; and now that they had been stirred to their inmost depths, it was no human voice that could still the tempest. It may be, however, that Cortés did not so much misconceive the character of the people. He may have felt that an authoritative tone was the only one he could assume with any chance of effect, in his present position, in which milder and more conciliatory language would, by intimating a consciousness of inferiority, have too certainly defeated its own object.

It was true, they answered, he had destroyed their temples, broken in pieces their gods, massacred their countrymen. Many more, doubtless, were yet to fall under their terrible swords. But they were content so long as for every thousand Mexicans they could shed the blood of a single white man! "Look out," they continued, "on our terraces and streets, see them still thronged with warriors as far as your eyes can reach. Our numbers are scarcely diminished by our losses. Yours, on the contrary, are lessening every hour. You are perishing from hunger and sickness. Your provisions and water are failing. You must soon fall into our hands. *The bridges are broken down, and you cannot escape!* There will be too few of you left to glut the vengeance of our Gods!" As they concluded, they sent a volley of arrows over the battlements, which compelled the Spaniards to descend and take refuge in their defences.

The fierce and indomitable spirit of the Aztecs filled the besieged with dismay. All, then, that they had done and suffered, their battles by day, their vigils by night, the perils they had braved, even the victories they had won, were of no avail. It was too evident that they had no longer the spring of ancient superstition to work upon, in the breasts of the natives, who, like some wild beast that has burst the bonds of his keeper, seemed now to swell and exult in the full consciousness of their strength. The annunciation respecting the bridges fell like a knell on the ears of the Christians. All that they had heard was too true, – and they gazed on one another with looks of anxiety and dismay.

The same consequences followed, which sometimes take place among the crew of a shipwrecked vessel. Subordination was lost in the dreadful sense of danger. A spirit of mutiny broke out, especially among the recent levies drawn from the army of Narvaez. They had come into the country from no motive of ambition, but attracted simply by the glowing reports of its opulence, and they had fondly hoped to return in a few months with their pockets well lined with the gold of the Aztec monarch. But how different had been their lot! From the first hour of their landing, they had experienced only trouble and disaster, privations of every description, sufferings unexampled, and they now beheld in perspective a fate yet more appalling. Bitterly did they lament the hour when they left the sunny fields of Cuba for these cannibal regions! And heartily did they curse their own folly in listening to the call of Velasquez, and still more, in embarking under the banner of Cortés!

They now demanded with noisy vehemence to be led instantly from the city, and refused to serve longer in defence of a place where they were cooped up like sheep in the shambles, waiting only to be dragged to slaughter. In all this they were rebuked by the more orderly soldierlike conduct of the veterans of Cortés. Those latter had shared with their general the day of his prosperity, and they were not disposed to desert him in the tempest. It was, indeed, obvious, on a little reflection, that the only chance of safety, in the existing crisis, rested on subordination and union; and that even this chance must be greatly diminished under any other leader than their present one.

Thus pressed by enemies without and by factions within, that leader was found, as usual, true to himself. Circumstances so appalling, as would have paralyzed a common mind, only stimulated his to higher action, and drew forth all its resources. He combined what is most rare, singular coolness and constancy of purpose, with a spirit of enterprise that might well be called romantic. His presence of mind did not now desert him. He calmly surveyed his condition, and weighed the difficulties which surrounded him, before coming to a decision. Independently of the hazard of a retreat in the face of a watchful and desperate foe, it was a deep mortification to surrender up the city, where he had so long lorded it as a master; to abandon the rich treasurers which he had secured to himself and his followers; to forego the very means by which he had hoped to propitiate the favor of his sovereign, and secure an amnesty for his irregular proceedings. This, he well knew must, after all, be dependent on success. To fly now was to acknowledge himself further removed from the conquest than ever. What a close was this to a career so auspiciously begun! What a contrast to his magnificent vaunts! What a triumph would it afford to his enemies! The governor of Cuba would be amply revenged.

But, if such humiliating reflections crowded on his mind, the alternative of remaining, in his present crippled condition, seemed yet more desperate. With his men daily diminishing in strength and numbers, their provisions reduced so low that a small daily ration of bread was all the sustenance afforded to the solider under his extraordinary fatigues, with the breaches every day widening in his feeble fortifications, with his ammunition, in fine, nearly expended, it would be impossible to maintain the place much longer – and none but men of iron constitutions and tempers, like the Spaniards, could have held it out so long – against the enemy. The chief embarrassment was as to the time and manner in which it would be expedient to evacuate the city. The best route seemed to be that of Tlacopan (Tacuba). For the causeway, the most dangerous part of the road, was but two miles long in that direction, and would, therefore, place the fugitives, much sooner than either of the other great avenues, on terra firma. Before his final departure, however, he proposed to make another sally in that direction, in order to reconnoitre the ground, and, at the same time, divert the enemy's attention from his real purpose by a show of active operations.

For some days his workmen had been employed in constructing a military machine of his own invention. It was called a *manta*, and was contrived somewhat on the principle of the mantelets used in the wars of the Middle Ages. It was, however, more complicated, consisting of a tower made of light beams and planks, having two chambers, one over the other. These were to be filled with musketeers, and the sides were provided with loop-holes, through which a fire could be kept up on the enemy. The great advantage proposed by this contrivance was, to accord a defence to the troops against the missiles hurled from the terraces. These machines, three of which were made rested on rollers, and were provided with strong ropes, by which they were to be dragged along the streets by the Tlascalan auxiliaries.

The Mexicans gazed with astonishment on this war-like machinery, and, as the rolling fortresses advanced, belching forth fire and smoke from their entrails, the enemy, incapable of making an impression on those within, fell back in dismay. By bringing the *mantas* under the walls of the houses, the Spaniards were enabled to fire with effect on the mischievous tenants of the *azoteas*, and when this did not silence them, by letting a ladder, or light drawbridge, fall on the roof from the top terrace of the *manta*, they opened a passage to the terrace, and closed with the combatants hand to hand. They could not, however, thus approach the higher buildings, from which the Indian warriors threw down such heavy masses of stone and timber as dislodged the planks that covered the machines, or, thundering against their sides, shook the frail edifices to their foundations, threatening all within with indiscriminate ruin. Indeed, the success of the experiment was doubtful, when the intervention of a canal put a stop to their further progress.

The Spaniards now found the assertion of their enemies too well confirmed. The bridge which traversed the opening had been demolished; and, although the canals which intersected the city were, in general, of no great width or depth, the removal of the bridges not only impeded the movements of the general's clumsy machines, but effectually disconcerted those of his cavalry. Resolving to abandon the *mantas*, he gave orders to fill up the chasm with stone, timber, and other rubbish drawn from the ruined buildings, and to make a new passage-way for the army. While this labor was going on, the Aztec slingers and archers on the other side of the opening kept up a galling discharge on the Christians, the more defenceless from the nature of their occupation. When the work was completed, and a safe passage secured, the Spanish cavaliers rode briskly against the enemy, who, unable to resist the shock of the steel-clad column, fell back with precipitation to where another canal afforded a similar strong position for defence.

There were no less than seven of these canals, intersecting the great street of Tlacopan, and at every one the same scene was renewed, the Mexicans making a gallant stand, and inflicting some loss, at each, on their persevering antagonists. These operations consumed two days, when, after incredible toil, the Spanish general had the satisfaction to find the line of communication completely reestablished through the whole length of the avenue, and the principal bridges placed under strong detachments of infantry. At this juncture, when he had driven the foe before him to the furthest extremity of the street, where it touches on the causeway, he was informed, that the Mexicans, disheartened by their reverses, desire to open a parley with him respecting the terms of accommodation, and that their chiefs awaited his return for that purpose at the fortress. Overjoyed at the intelligence, he instantly rode back, attended by Alvarado, Sandoval, and about sixty of the cavaliers, to his quarters.

The Mexicans proposed that he should release the two priests captured in the temple, who might be the bearers of his terms, and serve as agents for conducting the negotiations.

They were accordingly sent with the requisite instructions to their countrymen. But they did not return. The whole was an artifice of the enemy, anxious to procure the liberation of their religious leaders, one of whom was their *teoteuctli*, or high priest, whose presence was indispensable in the probable event of a new coronation.

Cortés, meanwhile, relying on the prospects of a speedy arrangement, was hastily taking some refreshment with his officers, after the fatigues of the day; when he received the alarming tidings, that the enemy were in arms again, with more fury than ever; that they had overpowered the detachments posted under Alvarado at three of the bridges, and were busily occupied in demolishing them. Stung with shame at the facility with which he had been duped by his wily foe, or rather by his own sanguine hopes, Cortés threw himself into the saddle, and, followed by his brave companions, galloped back at full speed to the scene of action. The Mexicans recoiled before the impetuous charge of the Spaniards. The bridges were again restored; and Cortés and his chivalry rode down the whole extent of the great street, driving the enemy, like frightened deer, at the points of their lances. But, before he could return on his steps, he had the mortification to find, that the indefatigable foe, gathering from the adjoining lanes and streets, had again closed on his infantry, who, worn down by fatigue, were unable to maintain their position, at one of the principal bridges. New swarms of warriors now poured in on all sides, overwhelming the little band of Christian cavaliers with a storm of stones, darts, and arrows, which rattled like hail on their armor and on that of their well-barbed horses. Most of the missiles, indeed, glanced harmless from the good panoplies of steel, or thick quilted cotton, but, now and then, one better aimed penetrated the joints of the harness, and stretched the rider on the ground.

The confusion became greater around the broken bridge. Some of the horsemen were thrown into the canal, and their steeds floundered wildly about without a rider. Cortés himself, at this crisis, did more than any other to cover the retreat of his followers. While the bridge was repairing, he plunged bolding into the midst of the barbarians, striking down an enemy at every vault of his charger, cheering on his own men, and spreading terror through the ranks of his opponents by the well-known sound of his battle-cry. Never did he display greater hardihood, or more freely expose his person, emulating, says an old chronicler, the feats of the Roman Cocles. In this way he stayed the tide of assailants, till the last man crossed the bridge, when, some of the planks having given way, he was compelled to leap a chasm of full six feet in width, amidst a cloud of missiles, before he could place himself in safety. A report ran through the army that the general was slain. It soon spread through the city, to the great joy of the Mexicans, and reached the fortress, where the besieged were thrown into no less consternation. But, happily for them, it was false. He, indeed received two severe contusions on the knee, but, in other respects remained uninjured. At no time, however, had he been in such extreme danger; and his escape, and that of his companions, were esteemed little less than a miracle.

The coming of night dispersed the Indian battalions, which, vanishing like birds of ill omen from the field, left the well-contested pass in possession of the Spaniards. They returned, however, with none of the joyous feelings of conquerors to their citadel, but with slow step and dispirited, with weapons hacked, armor battered, and fainting under the loss of blood, fasting, and fatigue. In this condition they had yet to learn the tidings of a fresh misfortune in the death of Montezuma.

The Indian monarch had rapidly declined, since he had received his injury, sinking, however, quite as much under the anguish of a wounded spirit, as under disease. He continued in the same moody state of insensibility as that already described; holding little communication with those around him, deaf to consolation, obstinately rejecting all medical remedies, as well as nourishment. Perceiving his end approach, some of the cavaliers present in the fortress, whom the kindness of his manners had personally attached to him, were anxious to save the soul of the dying prince from the sad doom of those who perish in the darkness of unbelief. They accordingly waited on him, with father Olmedo at their head, and in the most earnest manner implored him to open his eyes to the error of his creed, an consent to be baptized. But Montezuma – whatever may have been suggested to the contrary – seems never to have faltered in his hereditary faith, or to have contemplated becoming an apostate; for surely he merits that name in its most odious application, who, whether Christian or Pagan, renounces his religion without conviction of its falsehood. Indeed, it was a too implicit reliance on its oracles, which had led him to give such easy confidence to the Spaniards. His intercourse with them had, doubtless, not sharpened his desire to embrace their communion; and the calamities of his country he might consider as sent by his gods to punish him for his hospitality to those who had desecrated and destroyed their shrines.

When father Olmedo, therefore, kneeling at his side, with the uplifted crucifix, affectionately besought him to embrace the sign of man's redemption, he coldly repulsed the priest, exclaiming, "I have but a few moments to live; and will not at this hour desert the faith of my fathers." One thing, however, seemed to press heavily on Montezuma's mind. This was the fate of his children, especially of three daughters, whom he had by his two wives; for there were certain rites of marriage, which distinguished the lawful wife from the concubine. Calling Cortés to his bedside, he earnestly commended these children to his care, as "the most precious jewels that he could leave him." He besought the general to interest his master, the emperor, in their behalf, and to see that they should not be left destitute, but be allowed some portion of their rightful inheritance. "Your lord will do this," he concluded, "if it were only for the friendly offices I have rendered the Spaniards, and for the love I have shown them, – though it has brought me to this condition! But for this I bear them no ill-will." Such, according to Cortés himself, were the words of the dying monarch. Not long after, on the 30th of June, 1520, he expired in the arms of some of his own nobles, who still remained faithful in their attendance on his person. "Thus," exclaims a native historian, one of his enemies, a Tlascalan, "thus died the unfortunate Montezuma, who had swayed the sceptre with such consummate policy and wisdom; and who was held in greater reverence and awe than any other prince of his lineage, or indeed, that ever sat on a throne in this Western World. With him may be said to have terminated the royal line of the Aztecs, and the glory to have passed away from the empire, which under him had reached the zenith of its prosperity." "The tidings of his death," says the old Castilian chronicler, Diaz, "were received with real grief by every cavalier and solider in the army who had had access to his person; for we all loved him as a father, – and no wonder, seeing how good he was."

It is not easy to depict the portrait of Montezuma in its true colors, since it has been exhibited to us under two aspects, of the most opposite and contradictory character. In the accounts gathered of him by the Spaniards, on coming into the country, he was uniformly represented as bold and warlike, unscrupulous as to the means of gratifying his ambition, hollow and perfidious, the terror of his foes, with a haughty bearing which made him feared even by his own people. They found him, on the contrary, not merely affable and gracious, but disposed to waive all the advantages of his own position, and to place them on a footing with himself; making their wishes his law; gentle even to effeminacy in his deportment, and constant in his friendship, while his whole nation was in arms against them. – Yet these traits, so contradictory, were truly enough drawn. They are to be explained by the extraordinary circumstances of his position.

When Montezuma ascended the thrown, he was scarcely twenty-three years of age. Young, and ambitious of extending his empire, he was continually engaged in war, and is said to have been present himself in nine pitched battles. He was greatly renowned for his martial prowess, for he belonged to the *Quachictin*, the highest military order of his nation, and one into which but few even of its sovereigns had been admitted. In later life, he preferred intrigue to violence, as more consonant to his character and priestly education. In this he was as great an adept as any prince of his time, and, by arts not very honorable to himself, succeeded in filching away much of the territory of his royal kinsman of Tezcuco. Severe in the administration of justice, he made important reforms in the arrangement of the tribunals. He introduced other innovations in the royal household, creating new offices, introducing a lavish magnificence and forms of courtly etiquette unknown to his ruder predecessors. He was, in short, most attentive to all that concerned the exterior and pomp of royalty. Stately and decorous, he was careful of his own dignity, and might be said to be as great an "actor of majesty" among the barbarian potentates of the New World, as Louis the Fourteenth was among the polished princes of Europe.

He was deeply tinctured, moreover, with that spirit of bigotry, which threw such a shade over the latter days of the French monarch. He received the Spaniards as the beings predicted by his oracles. The anxious dread, with which he had evaded their proffered visit, was founded on the same feelings which led him so blindly to resign himself to them on their approach. He felt himself rebuked by their superior genius. He at once conceded all that they demanded, – his treasures, his power, even his person. For their sake, he forsook his wonted occupations, his pleasures, his most familiar habits. He might be said to forego his nature; and, as his subjects asserted, to change his sex and become a woman. If we cannot refuse our contempt for the pusillanimity of the Aztec monarch, it should be mitigated by the consideration, that his pusillanimity sprung from his superstition, and that superstition in the savage is the substitute for religious principle in the civilized man.

It is not easy to contemplate the fate of Montezuma without feelings of the strongest compassion; – to see him thus borne along the tide of events beyond his power to avert or control; to see him, like some stately tree, the pride of his own Indian forests, towering aloft in the pomp and majesty of its branches, by its very eminence a mark for the thunderbolt, the first victim of the tempest which was to sweep over it's native hills! When the wise king of Tezcuco addressed his royal relative at his coronation he exclaimed, "Happy the empire, which is now in the meridian of its prosperity, for the sceptre is given to one whom the Almighty has in his keeping; and the nations shall hold him in reverence!" Alas! the subject of this auspicious invocation lived to see his empire melt away like the winter's wreath; to see a strange race drop, as it were from the clouds, on his land; to find himself a prisoner in the palace of his fathers, the companion of those who were the enemies of his gods and his people; to be insulted, reviled, trodden in the dust, by the meanest of his subjects, by those who, a few months previous, had trembled at his glance; drawing his last breath in the halls of the stranger, a lonely outcast in the heart of his own capital! He was the sad victim of destiny, – a destiny as dark and irresistible in its march, as that which broods over the mythic legends of Antiquity!

Montezuma, at the time of his death, was about forty-one years old, of which he reigned eighteen. His person and manners have been already described. He left a numerous progeny by his various wives, most of whom, having lost their consideration after the Conquest, fell into obscurity, as they mingled with the mass of the Indian population. Two of them, however, a son and a daughter, who embraced, Christianity, became the founders of noble houses in Spain. The government, willing to show its gratitude for the large extent of empire derived from their ancestor, conferred on them ample estates, and important hereditary honors; and the Counts of Montezuma and Tula, intermarrying with the best blood of Castile, intimated by their names and titles their illustrious descent from the royal dynasty of Mexico.

Montezuma's death was a misfortune to the Spaniards. While he lived, they had a precious pledge in their hands, which, in extremity, they might possibly have turned to account. Now the last link was snapped which connected them with the natives of the country. But independently of interested feelings, Cortés and his officers were much affected by his death from personal considerations; and, when they gazed on the cold remains of the ill-starred monarch, they may have felt a natural compunction, as they contrasted his late flourishing condition with that to which his friendship for them had now reduced him.

The Spanish commander showed all respect for his memory. His body, arrayed in its royal robes, was laid decently on a bier, and borne on the shoulders of his nobles to his subjects in the city. What honors, if any, indeed, were paid to his remains, is uncertain. A sound of wailing, distinctly heard in the western quarters of the capital, was interpreted by the Spaniards into the moans of a funeral procession, as it bore the body to be laid among those of his ancestors, under the princely shades of Chapoltepec. Others state, that it was removed to a burial-place in the city named Copalco, and there burnt with the usual solemnities and signs of lamentations by his chiefs, but not without some unworthy insults from the Mexican populace. Whatever be the fact, the people, occupied with the stirring scenes in which they were engaged, were probably not long mindful of the monarch, who had taken no share in their late patriotic movements. Nor is it strange that the very memory of his sepulchre should be effaced in the terrible catastrophe which afterwards overwhelmed the capital, and swept away every landmark from its surface.

There was no longer any question as to the expediency of evacuating the capital. The only doubt was as to the time of doing so, and the route. There was some difference of opinion in respect to the hour of departure. The day-time, it was argued by some, would be preferable, since it would enable them to see the nature and extent of their danger, and to provide against it. Darkness would be much more likely to embarrass their own movements than those of the enemy, who were familiar with the ground. A thousand impediments would occur in the night, which might prevent their acting in concert, or obeying, or even ascertaining, the orders of the commander. But, on the other hand, it was urged, that the night presented many obvious advantages in dealing with a foe who rarely carried his hostilities beyond the day. The late active operations of the Spaniards had thrown the Mexicans off their guard, and it was improbable they would anticipate so speedy a departure of their enemies. With celerity and caution, they might succeed, therefore, in making their escape from the town, possibly over the causeway, before their retreat should be discovered; and, could they once get beyond that pass of peril, they felt little apprehension for the rest. At all events, it was decided to abandon the city that very night.

The general's first care was to provide for the safe transportation of the treasure. Many of the common soldiers had converted their share of the prize, as we have seen, into gold chains, collars, or other ornaments, which they easily carried about their persons. But the royal fifth, together with that of Cortés himself, and much of the rich booty of the principal cavaliers, had been converted into bars and wedges of solid gold, and deposited in one of the strong apartments of the palace. Cortés delivered the share belonging to the Crown to the royal officers, assigning them one of the strongest horses, and a guard of Castilian soldiers, to transport it. Still, much of the treasure, belonging both to the Crown and to individuals, was necessarily abandoned, from the want of adequate means of conveyance. The metal lay scattered in shining heaps along the floor, exciting the cupidity of the soldiers. "Take what you will of it," said Cortés to his men. "Better you should have it, than these Mexican hounds. But be careful not to overload yourselves. He travels safest in the dark night who travels lightest." His own more wary followers took heed to his counsels, helping themselves to a few articles of least bulk, though, it might be, of greatest value. But the troops of Narvaez, pining for riches, of which they had heard so much, and hitherto seen so little, showed no such discretion. To them it seemed as if the very mines of Mexico were turned up before them, and, rushing to the treacherous spoil, they greedily loaded themselves with as much of it, not merely as they could accommodate about their persons, but as they could stow away in wallets, boxes, or any other mode of conveyance at their disposal.

Cortés next arranged the order of march. The van composed of two hundred Spanish foot, he placed under the command of the valiant Gonzalo de Sandoval, supported by

Diego de Ordaz, Francisco de Lujo, and about twenty other cavaliers. The rearguard, constituting the strength of the infantry, was intrusted to Pedro de Alvarado, and Velasquez de Leon. The general himself took charge of the "battle", or centre, in which went the baggage, some of the heavy guns, most of which, however, remained in the rear, the treasure, and the prisoners. These consisted of a son and two daughters of Montezuma, Cacama, the deposed lord of Tezcuco, and several other nobles, whom Cortés retained as important pledges in his future negotiations with the enemy. The Tlascalans were distributed pretty equally among the three divisions; and Cortés had under his immediate command a hundred picked soldiers, his own veterans most attached to his service, who, with Christoval de Olid, Francisco de Morla, Alonso de Avila, and two or three other cavaliers, formed a select corps, to act wherever occasion might require.

The general had already superintended the construction of a portable bridge to be laid over the open canals in the causeway. This was given in charge to an officer named Magarino, with forty soldiers under his orders, all pledged to defend the passage to the last extremity. The bridge was to be taken up when the entire army had crossed one of the breaches, and transported to the next. There were three of these openings in the causeway, and most fortunate would it have been for the expedition, if the foresight of the commander had provided the same number of bridges. But the labor would have been great, and time was short.

At midnight the troops were under arms, in readiness for the march. Mass was performed by father Olmedo, who invoked the protection of the Almighty through the awful perils of the night. The gates were thrown open, and, on the first of July, 1520, the Spaniards for the last time sallied forth from the walls of the ancient fortress, the scene of so much suffering and such indomitable courage.

The night was cloudy, and a drizzling rain, which feel without intermission, added to the obscurity. The great square before the palace was deserted, as, indeed, it had been since the fall of Montezuma. Steadily, and as noiselessly as possible, the Spaniards held their way along the great street of Tlacopan, which so lately had resounded in the tumult of battle. All was now hushed in silence; and they were only reminded of the past by the occasional presence of some solitary corpse, or a dark heap of the slain, which too plainly told where the strife had been hottest. As they passed along the lanes and alleys which opened into the great street, or looked down the canals, whose polished surface gleamed with a sort of ebon lustre through the obscurity of the night, they easily fancied that they discerned the shadowy forms of their foe lurking in ambush, and ready to spring on them. But it was only fancy; and the city slept undisturbed even by the prolonged echoes of the tramp of the horses, and the hoarse rumbling of the artillery and baggage trains. At length a lighter space beyond the dusky line of buildings showed the van of the army that it was emerging on the open causeway. They might well have congratulated themselves on having thus escaped the dangers of an assault in the city itself, and that a brief time would place them in comparative safety on the opposite shore. – But the Mexicans were not all asleep.

As the Spaniards drew near the spot where the street opened on the causeway, and were preparing to lay the portable bridge across the uncovered breach, which now met their eyes, several Indian sentinels, who had been stationed at this, as at the other approaches to the city, took the alarm, and fled, rousing their countrymen by their cries. The priests, keeping their night watch on the summit of the *teocallis*, instantly caught the tidings and sounded their shells, while the huge drum in the desolate temple of the war-god sent forth those solemn tones, which, heard only in seasons of calamity, vibrated through every corner of the capital. The Spaniards saw that no time was to be lost. The bridge was brought forward and fitted with all possible expedition. Sandoval was the first to try its strength, and, riding across, was followed by his little body of chivalry, his infantry, and Tlasclan allies, who formed the first division of the army. Then came Cortés and his squadrons, with the baggage, ammunition wagons, and a part of the artillery. But before they had time to defile across the narrow passage, a gathering sound was heard, like that of a mighty forest agitated by the winds. It grew louder and louder, while on the dark waters of the lake was heard a plashing noise, as of many oars. Then came a few stones and arrows striking at random among the hurrying troops. They feel every moment faster and more furious, till they thickened into a terrible tempest, while the very heavens were rent with the yells and war-cries of myriads of combatants, who seemed all at once to be swarming over land and lake!

The Spaniards pushed steadily on through this arrowy sleet, though the barbarians, dashing their canoes against the sides of the causeway, clambered up and broke in upon their ranks. But the Christians, anxious only to make their escape, declined all combat except for self-preservation. The cavaliers, spurring forward their steeds, shook off their assailants, and rode over their prostate bodies, while the men on foot with their good swords or the butts of their pieces drove them headlong again down the sides of the dike.

But the advance of several thousand men, marching, probably, on a front of not more than fifteen or twenty abreast, necessarily required much time, and the leading files had already reached the second breach in the causeway before those in the rear had entirely traversed the first. Here they halted; as they had no means of effecting a passage, smarting all the while under unintermitting volleys from the enemy, who were clustered thick on the waters around this second opening. Sorely distressed, the van-guard sent repeated messages to the rear to demand the portable bridge. At length the last of the army had crossed, and Magarino and his sturdy followers endeavoured to raise the ponderous framework. But it struck fast in the sides of the dike. In vain they strained every nerve. The weight of so many men and horses, and above all of the heavy artillery, had wedged the timbers so firmly in the stones and earth, that it was beyond their power to dislodge them. Still they labored amidst a torrent of missiles, until, many of them slain, and all wounded, they were obliged to abandon the attempt.

The tidings soon spread from man to man, and no sooner was their dreadful import comprehended, than a cry of despair arose, which for a moment drowned all the noise of conflict. All means of retreat were cut off. Scarcely hope was left. The only hope was in such desperate exertions as each could make for himself. Order and subordination were at an end. Intense danger produced intense selfishness. Each thought only of his own life. Pressing forward, he trampled down the weak and the wounded, heedless, whether it were friend or foe. The leading files, urged on by the rear, were crowded on the brink of the gulf. Sandoval, Ordaz, and the other cavaliers dashed into the water. Some succeeded in swimming their horses across. Other failed, and some, who reached the opposite bank, being overturned in the ascent, rolled headlong with their steeds into the lake. The infantry followed pellmell, heaped promiscuously on one another, frequently pierced by the shafts, or struck down by the war-clubs of the Aztecs; while many an unfortunate victim was dragged half-stunned on board their canoes, to be reserved for a protracted, but more dreadful death.

The carnage raged fearfully along the length of the causeway. Its shadowy bulk presented a mark of sufficient distinctness for the enemy's missiles, which often prostrated their own countrymen in the blind fury of the tempest. Those nearest the dike, running their canoes alongside, with a force that shattered them to pieces, leaped on the land, and grappled with the Christians, until both came rolling down the side of the causeway together. But the Aztec fell among his friends, while his antagonist was borne away in triumph to the sacrifice. The struggle was long and deadly. The Mexicans were recognized by their white cotton tunics, which showed faint through the darkness. Above the combatants rose a wild and discordant clamor, in which horrid shouts of vengeance were mingled with groans of agony, with invocations of the saints and the blessed Virgin, and with the screams of women; for there were several women, both native and Spaniards, who have accompanied the Christian camp. Among these, one named Maria de Estrada is particularly noticed for the courage she displayed, battling with broadsword and target like the stanchest of the warriors.

The opening in the causeway, meanwhile, was filled up with the wreck of matter which had been forced into it, ammunition-waggons, heavy guns, bales of rich stuffs scattered over the waters, chests of solid ingots, and bodies of men and horses, till over this dismal ruin a passage was gradually formed, by which those in the rear were enabled to clamber to the other side. Cortés, it is said, found a place that was fordable, where, halting, with the water up to his saddle-girths, he endeavoured to check the confusion, and lead his followers by a safer path to the opposite bank. But his voice was lost in the wild uproar, and finally, hurrying on with the tide, he pressed forwards with a few trusty cavaliers, who remained near his person, to the van; but not before he had seen his favorite page, Juan de Salazar, struck down, a corpse, by his side. Here he found Sandoval and his companions, halting before the third and last breach, endeavouring to cheer on their followers to surmount it. But their resolution faltered. It was wide and deep; though the passage was not so closely beset by the enemy as the preceding ones. The cavaliers again set the example by plunging into the water. Horse and foot followed as they could, some swimming, others with dying grasp clinging to the manes and tails of the struggling animals. Those fared best, as the general had predicted, who travelled lightest; and many were the unfortunate wretches, who, weighed down by the fatal gold which they loved so well, were buried with it in the salt floods of the lake. Cortés with his gallant comrades, Olid, Morla, Sandoval, and some few others, still kept in the advance, leading his broken remnant off the fatal causeway. The din of battle lessened in the distance; when the rumor reached them, that the rearguard would be wholly overwhelmed without speedy relief. It seemed almost an act of desperation; but the generous hearts of the Spanish cavaliers did not stop to calculate danger, when the cry for succour reached them. Turning their horses' bridles, they galloped back to the theatre of action, worked their way through the press, swam the canal, and placed themselves in the thick of the *mêlée* on the opposite bank.

The first grey of the morning was now coming over the waters. It showed the hideous confusion of the scene which had been shrouded in the obscurity of night. The dark masses of combatants, stretching along the dike, were seen struggling for mastery, until the very causeway on which they stood, appeared to tremble, and reel to and fro, as if shaken by an earthquake; while the bosom of the lake, as far as the eye could reach, was darkened by canoes crowded with warriors, whose spears and bludgeons, armed with blades of "volcanic glass," gleamed in the morning light.

The cavaliers found Alvarado unhorsed, and defending himself with a poor handful of followers against an overwhelming tide of the enemy. His good steed, which had borne him through many a hard fight, had fallen under him. He was himself wounded in several places, and was striving in vain to rally his scattered column, which was driven to the verge of the canal by the fury of the enemy, then in possession of the whole rear of the causeway, where they were reinforced every hour by fresh combatants from the city. The artillery in the earlier part of the engagement had not been idle, and its iron shower, sweeping along the dike, had mowed down the assailants by hundreds. But nothing could resist their impetuosity. The front ranks, pushed on by those behind, were at length forced up to the pieces, and pouring over them like a torrent, overthrew men and guns in one general ruin. The resolute charge of the Spanish cavaliers, who had now arrived, created a temporary check, and gave time for their countrymen to make a feeble rally. But they were speedily borne down by the returning flood. Cortés and his companions were compelled to plunge again into the lake, – though all did not escape. Alvarado stood on the brink for a moment, hesitating what to do. Unhorsed as he was, to throw himself into the water in the face of the hostile canoes that now swarmed around the opening, afforded but a desperate chance of safety. He had but a second for thought. He was a man of powerful frame, and despair gave him unnatural energy. Setting his long lance firmly on the wreck which strewed the bottom of the lake, he sprung forward with all his might, and cleared the wide gap at a leap! Aztecs and Tlascalans gazed in stupid amazement, exclaiming, as they beheld the incredible feat, "This is truly the *Tonatiuh*, – the child of the Sun!" – The breadth of the opening is not given. But it was so great, that the valorous captain Diaz, who well remembered the place, says the leap was impossible to any man. Other contemporaries, however, do not discredit the story. It was, beyond doubt, matter of popular belief at the time; it is to this day familiarly known to every inhabitant of the capital; and the name of the *Salto de Alvarado*, "Alvarado's Leap," given to the spot, still commemorates an exploit which rivalled those of the demigods of Grecian fable.

Cortés and his companions now rode forward to the front, where the troops, in a loose, disorderly manner, were marching off the fatal causeway. A few only of the enemy hung on their rear, or annoyed them by occasional flights of arrows from the lake. The attention of the Aztecs was diverted by the rich spoil that strewed the battle-ground; fortunately for the Spaniards, who, had their enemy pursued with the same ferocity with which he had fought, would, in their crippled condition, have been cut off, probably, to a man. But little molested, therefore, they were allowed to defile through the adjacent village, or suburbs, it might be called, of Popotla.

The Spanish commander there dismounted from his jaded steed, and sitting down on the steps of an Indian temple, gazed mournfully on the broken files as they passed before him. What a spectacle did they present! The cavalry, most of them dismounted, were mingled with the infantry, who dragged their feeble limbs long with difficulty; their shattered mail and tattered garments dripping with the salt ooze, showing through their rents many a bruise and ghastly wound; their bright arms soiled, their proud crests and banners gone, the baggage, artillery, all, in short, that constitutes the pride and panoply of glorious war, for ever lost. Cortés, as he looked wistfully on their thinned and disordered ranks, sought in vain for many a familiar face, and missed more than one dear companion who had stood side by side with him through all the perils of the Conquest. Though accustomed to control his emotions, or, at least, to conceal them, the sight was too much for him. He covered his face with his hands, and the tears, which trickled down, revealed too plainly the anguish of his soul.

He found some consolation, however, in the sight of several of the cavaliers on whom he most relied. Alvarado, Sandoval, Olid, Ordaz, Avila, were yet safe. He had the inexpressible satisfaction, also, of learning the safety of the

Indian interpreter, Marina, so dear to him, and so important to the army. She had been committed with a daughter of a Tlascalan chief, to several of that nation. She was fortunately placed in the van and her faithful escort had carried her securely through all the dangers of the night. Aguilar, the other interpreter, had also escaped. And it was with no less satisfaction, that Cortés learned the safety of the ship-builder, Martin Lopez. The general's solicitude for the fate of this man, so indispensable, as he proved, to the success of his subsequent operations, showed that, amidst all his affliction, his indomitable spirit was looking forward to the hour of vengeance.

Meanwhile, the advancing column had reached the neighbouring city of Tlacopan, (Tacuba,) once the capital of an independent principality. There it halted in the great street, as if bewildered and altogether uncertain what course to take; like a herd of panic-struck deer, who, flying from the hunters, with the cry of hound and horn still ringing from their ears, look wildly around for some glen or copse in which to plunge for concealment. Cortés, who had hastily mounted and rode on to the front again, saw the danger of remaining in a populous place, where the inhabitants might sorely annoy the troops from the *azoteas*, with little risk to themselves. Pushing forward, therefore, he soon led them into the country. There he endeavoured to reform his disorganized battalions, and bring them to something like order.

Hard by, at no great distance on the left, rose an eminence, looking towards a chain of mountains which fences in the Valley on the west. It was called the Hill of Otoncalpolco, and sometimes the Hill of Montezuma. It was crowned with an Indian *teocalli*, with its large outworks of stone covering an ample space, and by its strong position, which commanded the neighbouring plain, promised a good place of refuge for the exhausted troops. But the men, disheartened and stupefied by their late reverses, seemed for the moment incapable of further exertion; and the place was held by a body of armed Indians. Cortés saw the necessity of dislodging them, if he would save the remains of his army from entire destruction. The event showed he still held a control over their wills stronger than circumstances themselves. Cheering them on, and supported by his gallant cavaliers, he succeeded in infusing into the most sluggish something of his own intrepid temper, and led them up the ascent in face of the enemy. But the latter made slight resistance, and, after a few feeble volleys of missiles which did little injury, left the ground to the assailants.

It was covered by a building of considerable size, and furnished ample accommodations for the diminished numbers of the Spaniards. They found there some provisions; and more, it is said, were brought to them, in the course of the day, from some friendly Otomie villages in the neighbourhood. There was, also a quantity of fuel in the courts, destined to the uses of the temple. With this they made fires to dry their drenched garments, and busily employed themselves in dressing one another's wounds, stiff and extremely painful from exposure and long exertion. Thus refreshed, the weary soldiers threw themselves down on the floor and courts of the temple, and soon found the temporary oblivion, – which Nature seldom denies even in the greatest extremity of suffering.

There was one eye in that assembly, however, which we may well believe did not so speedily close. For what agitating thoughts must have crowded in on the mind of their commander, as he beheld his poor remnant of followers thus huddled together in this miserable bivouac! And this was all that survived of the brilliant array with which but a few weeks since he had entered the capital of Mexico! Where now were his dreams of conquest and empire? And what was he but a luckless adventurer, at whom the finger of scorn would be uplifted as a madman? Whichever way he turned, the horizon was almost equally gloomy, with scarcely one light spot to cheer him. He had still a weary journey before him, through perilous and unknown paths, with guides of whose fidelity he could not be assured. And how could he rely on his reception at Tlascala, the place of his destination; the land of his ancient enemies; where, formerly as a foe, and now as a friend, he had brought desolation to every family within its borders?

The loss sustained by the Spaniards on this fatal night, like every other event in the history of the Conquest, is reported with the greatest discrepancy. If we believe Cortés' own letter, it did not exceed one hundred and fifty Spaniards and two thousand Indians. But the general's bulletins, while they do full justice to the difficulties to be overcome, and the importance of the results are less scrupulous in stating the extent either of his means or his losses. Thoan Cano, one of the cavaliers present, estimates the slain at eleven hundred and seventy Spaniards, and eight thousand allies. But this is a greater number than we have allowed for the whole army. Perhaps we may come nearest the truth by taking the computation of Gomara, the chaplain of Cortés, who had free access, doubtless, not only to the general's papers, but to other authentic sources of information. According to him, the number of Christians killed and missing was four hundred and fifty, and that of natives four thousand. This, with the loss sustained in the conflicts of the previous week, may have reduced the former to something more than a third, and the latter to a fourth, or, perhaps, fifth, of the original force with which they entered the capital. The brunt of the action fell on the rear-guard, few of whom escaped. It was formed chiefly of the soldiers of Narvaez, who fell the victims in some measure of their cupidity. Forty-six of the cavalry were cut off, which with previous losses reduced the number in this branch of the service to twenty-three, and some of these in very poor condition. The greater part of the treasure, the baggage, the general's papers, including his accounts, and a minute diary of transactions since leaving Cuba, – which, to posterity, at least, would have been of more worth than the gold, – had been swallowed up by the waters. The ammunition, the beautiful little train of artillery, with which Cortés had entered the city, were all gone. Not a musket even remained, the men having thrown them away, eager to disencumber themselves of all that might retard their escape on that disastrous night. Nothing, in short, of their military apparatus was left, but their swords, their crippled cavalry, and a few damaged crossbows, to assert the superiority of the European over the barbarian.

The prisoners, including the children of Montezuma and the cacique of Tezcuco, all perished by the hands of their ignorant countrymen, it is said, in the indiscriminate fury of the assault. There were, also, some persons of consideration among the Spaniards, whose names were inscribed on the same bloody roll of slaughter. Such was Francisco de Morla, who fell by the side of Cortés, on returning with him to the rescue. But the greatest loss was that of Juan Velasquez de Leon, who, with Alvarado, had command of the rear. It was the post of danger on that night, and he fell bravely defending it, at an early hour of the retreat. He was an excellent officer, possessed of many knightly qualities, though somewhat haughty in his bearing, being one of the best connected cavaliers in the army. The near relation of the governor of Cuba, he looked coldly, at first, on the pretensions of Cortés; but, whether from a conviction that the latter had been wronged, or from personal preference, he afterwards attached himself zealously to his leader's interests. The general requited this with a generous confidence, assigning him, as we have seen, a separate and independent command, where misconduct, or even a mistake, would have been fatal to the expedition. Velasquez proved himself worthy of the trust; and there was no cavalier in the army, with the exception, perhaps, of Sandoval and Alvarado, whose loss would have been so deeply deplored by the commander. Such were the disastrous results of this terrible passage of the causeway; more disastrous than those occasioned by any other reverse which has stained the Spanish arms in the New World; and which have branded the night on which it happened, in the national annals, with the name of the *noche triste*, "the sad or melancholy night."